I'VE HAD SO MANY OF HIS WORKS. I'D SEE THEM IN THE MORNING WHEN I GOT UP AND BEFORE I WENT TO SLEEP. SOMETIMES I'D TAKE MY FLASHLIGHT TO SEE WHAT WAS GOING ON IN THE DARK. A LOT OF THEM CAN BE UNATTRACTIVE ON THE SURFACE. . .BUT YOU'VE GOT TO GET AWAY FROM THE OBVIOUS TO FIGURE IT OUT.

— JAMES F. DUFFY JR.

Gordon Newton

SELECTIONS FROM THE JAMES F. DUFFY JR. GIFT

THE DETROIT INSTITUTE OF ARTS

This catalogue is published in conjunction with the exhibition "Gordon Newton: Selections from the James F. Duffy Jr. Gift" at the Detroit Institute of Arts, July 15–November 4, 2001.

The exhibition was organized by the Detroit Institute of Arts and was made possible by funds from Lila and Gilbert B. Silverman, the Michigan Council for Arts and Cultural Affairs, and the City of Detroit.

CURATORS OF THE EXHIBITION: Nancy Sojka and MaryAnn Wilkinson

DIRECTOR OF PUBLICATIONS: Julia P. Henshaw

EDITOR: Judith Ruskin

DIRECTOR OF VISUAL RESOURCES: Dirk Bakker

GRAPHIC DESIGN: Ellen Wall, Letterspace Graphic Design

ISBN 0-8955-8157-4

Library of Congress Cataloging-in-Publications Data is available.
Printed and bound in the United States of America

Table of Contents

Untitled, 1974, 26 x 34 in., paint, crayon, graphite, and collage, including tape (1999.386).

Foreword

Gordon Newton: Selections from the James F. Duffy Jr. Gift provides the all too rare opportunity to study thirty years of an artist's work, from his earliest black-and-white abstract drawings to the heavily layered, richly colored figurative images made within the past decade.

Gordon Newton has been making art in Detroit since the late 1960s, and James F. Duffy Jr. has been acquiring his art for almost as long. Jim Duffy has, accordingly, amassed an unparalleled collection of Newton's work, in all media and from all periods of the artist's career. Over the years their relationship has developed into one of friendship.

Jim has also been a generous friend to the Detroit Institute of Arts. This exhibition is the direct result of his donation of a substantial body of Gordon Newton's works on paper. The more than five hundred drawings and forty sketchbooks give added dimension to the holdings of the artist's work already in the collection through purchase as well as earlier gifts from Jim, and from a number of other patrons.

This exhibition, part of the museum's ongoing support of Detroit artists, resulted from the collaboration between two curators from different departments: Nancy Sojka, associate curator of graphic arts, and MaryAnn Wilkinson, curator of modern and contemporary art. I thank them for putting together this celebration of the James F. Duffy Jr. gift—a very appropriate salute to one of Detroit's most devoted collectors and one of the city's finest artists—during this city's tricentennial year.

Thanks are also due the following museum staff members: Judith Ruskin, editor of this catalogue; Robert Hensleigh and Eric Wheeler, photographers; Doug Bulka and Jim Johnson, preparators; Valerie Baas and Christopher Foster, conservators; Pam Watson, Roberta Frey Gilboe, and Orian O'Meara, registrars; and Matthew Fry, communications specialist.

The contributions of several individuals made this book possible: Marsha Miro, author, who drew on her years as an art critic and reporter of the local art scene to trace Gordon Newton's career from his Cass Corridor days to the present; Ellen Wall, who designed this publication; and Lila and Gilbert B. Silverman, whose support allowed us to publish such a substantial book.

Finally, of course, particular thanks go to the artist for his work with the curators and authors in the formation of this exhibition and catalogue.

GRAHAM W. J. BEAL
DIRECTOR, THE DETROIT INSTITUTE OF ARTS

Channel Eight, 1978, 29 x 23 1/8 in., graphite, crayon, paint, wax, varnish, and collage (1999.216).

Knowing Gordon Newton

ATYPICAL

BREATHTAKING

COLLECTOR

DEEP

ENLIGHTENED

FAVORED

GIFTED

HONEST

INFORMED

JUDICIOUS

KINDLY

LARGE-MINDED

MYSTERIOUS

NATURAL

OPTIMISTIC

PERCEPTIVE

QUALITY

RESPONSIBILITY

SCHOLARLY

TALENT

UNIQUE

VALIANT

WIZARD

Poor X and Y and Z. We would have to go to Science.

James F. Duffy Jr.

GORDON NEWTON
THIRTY YEARS LATER

MARSHA MIRO

FIGURE 1: **Untitled,** 1972 (Plate 19).

GORDON NEWTON: THIRTY YEARS LATER

WHAT WE WERE DOING WAS A
CELEBRATION OF LIFE, AS SIMPLE
AS THAT. . .WE WERE ALL JUST
MAKING THINGS.

— GORDON NEWTON

GORDON NEWTON: THIRTY YEARS LATER

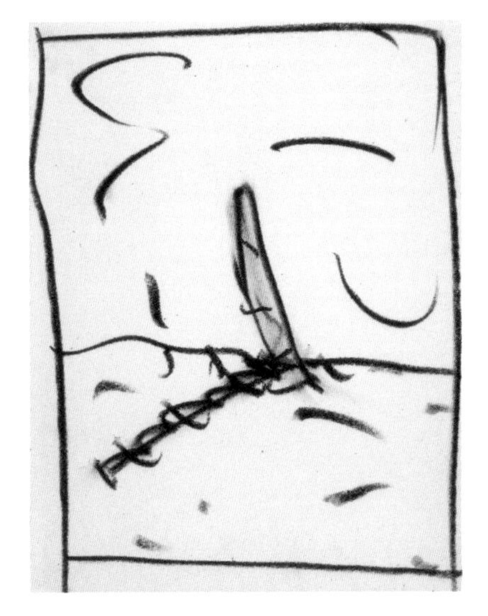

FIGURE 2: **Untitled**, 1970, (Plate 1).

Gordon Newton's art of the last three decades is complex, beautiful in unexpected ways, and always provocative. He has long understood how to use abstract expressionism, minimalist geometry, and various other visual languages together to deepen a work's intensity. Through the years, the principal supporter of Newton and his art has been James F. Duffy Jr., whose generous gift to the Detroit Institute of Arts of more than five hundred drawings and forty sketchbooks has made possible a study of the artist's work on paper from throughout his career. Seeing together Newton's lithographic crayon drawings of 1970 (see fig. 2) and the figurative works from the early 1990s (see fig. 3) is to understand that the forceful outlines of the images in the later work have the same brisk intensity of the mark making in his early abstract pieces. Newton's art has evolved with consistency. He is an intuitive artist, who knows where to find what he needs, having a voracious appetite for information, ideas, and materials.

Newton's handling of unconventional materials is crucial to the understanding of his art. Almost any material—new, used, or found, whole or dissected—could be incorporated to load a work with ideas, chance occurrences, and huge variety, increasing its tactility and sensuality. Newton substitutes jigsaws, drills, and flame for the traditional artist's brush to explore the imprint of the outside world on the nature of his creations. While increasing his vocabulary with the different marks made by these devices, he narrowed the gap in his work between art and life. Using this unusual assortment of tools and materials, he drew, painted, collaged, and built assemblages, sometimes all in one work, further enlarging the pool of variables from which he chose.

Over the years, Newton has explored industrial imagery, social problems, dimensions of time, motion, energy, cultural phenomena, natural cycles, games of chance, and technology—all within a conceptual framework. Mixing architectural concerns, sculpture, painting, the popular arts, and literary references is a constant. While he has moved from subject to subject, ever-present has been his connection to the environment, either rural or urban. An apocryphal edge hangs over most of his imagery, perhaps in part the residue of living in Detroit during unsettling times, when racial tensions and the ups and downs of the auto industry thrashed the population about on an emotional and economic roller coaster. Newton sucks in this darkness, letting it loose in the indigo that rampages through the marks and atmosphere of his images. One can't help but think about the power of industry diminished, of a place that was once a center but, like so many places before, forced to subsist on the whims of something, or someone, that cannot be controlled. The poignancy and potency of such a state infects his work.

FIGURE 3: **Untitled,** 1994 (Plate 102).

Newton moves from thoughts about things outside himself to examine interior forces, something he did with obsessive thoroughness in his lexicon of expressionistic heads of the 1990s (see fig. 3). Even his geometric collages have an expressionistic aspect in the implied motion of clashing and overlaid forms (see fig. 4). In direct and evocative ways, he physically conveys the connections among hand, heart, and paper. While personal concerns are present, they are deeply buried, with perhaps the only evidence on the surface being his obsessions.

He makes hundreds of studies to explore every aspect of an idea for a major piece. He then works these drawings over and over, building thick, dense surfaces, which take hundreds of hours to accumulate. He doesn't stop until he has exhausted an idea, having explored every nook and cranny of the variations. The quality of the work, the fresh way Newton brings together all these opposing forces and variables, folding in layer after layer of metaphor, reveals much of the nature of living. He believes in art as a way of learning, knowing, and experiencing: "It's like opening a book."[1]

Born in Detroit in 1948, Gordon Newton spent much of his childhood moving from one place to another. His parents, who are Canadian, took the family from Plymouth, Michigan, to Canton, Ohio, to Kansas then back to Michigan, finally settling in Port Huron. It was there, during the late 1960s, that Newton took art courses, crystallizing his decision to become an artist. Newton enrolled in classes taught by Vincent McPharlin, whose painting courses were held in the Port Huron Community College boathouse on Lake Huron, and with Earl Robinette, a painter and ceramic artist. McPharlin "was always doing landscapes," Newton recalls, and for his classes "we'd have to do still lives and landscapes. They were exercises. I always liked it." McPharlin's commitment to transcribing the outside world into paint inspired Newton.

Robinette, who taught Newton in 1967 and '68, remembers the artist as "one of a kind. He has a very subtle wit. I saw something about him that set him apart from the other students. His work was traditional at that time, but very creative. . . I told him 'Don't ever change; just go your own way.'

He was never afraid of trying anything, like the way he was putting odd stuff together that you never saw together then. He never paid much attention to danger. He'd try anything and worry about it afterwards."[2] In 1969 Newton left Port Huron for Detroit, enrolling in the art school of the Society of Arts and Crafts (now the Center for Creative Studies). While there, he joined with others in the growing artists' community in Detroit's Cass Corridor, not far from Wayne State University. The city's burgeoning art scene developed on either side of Cass Avenue, bordered on the east by Woodward Avenue and on the west by the Lodge expressway. The area was particularly hard hit by the social upheaval and general decline that affected the city as a whole. The riots of 1967 resulted in a new edginess, accompanied by a political agenda based on overcoming social inequalities. The emerging counterculture of the 1960s, with its protests, dropouts, and drugs, added a sense of both lawlessness and freedom, as it spread the belief that individuals could shape things as they pleased. The convergence of these forces, in the cultural center of Detroit where rents were cheap, brought together artists, poets, and musicians, creating a potent avant-garde arts scene in the city, probably for the first time.

"Kick Out the Jams: Detroit's Cass Corridor, 1963–1977," a 1980 exhibition at the Detroit Institute of Arts, attempted to codify the area's activities, but things were more unruly than any show could reconcile. The variousness of what was happening, the number of artists working in different modes and living in warehouses, apartment buildings, and offices, was overshadowed by something that became known as the Cass Corridor style, which, at the core, was an early strain of Neo-Expressionism.[3] The artists, many of whom made both paintings and three-dimensional objects, drew images out of emotional abstractions and gave the geometric an intensely emotional base with metaphorical associations. Their work was grounded in the rough, material culture of a declining industrial center. Place was critical; the aesthetic was tough. Some of the art was about destruction. Nearly all of it was about reconstruction, collaging, assembling, and melding together the disparate aspects of this world. Newton, described as "hard-living and intense," became, in the eyes of the art establishment, the prototypical Cass Corridor artist, rejecting "the conventional art world and the work it touted."[4]

FIGURE 4: **Untitled,** 1974 (Plate 21).

By the spring of 1969, Newton had left Arts and Crafts because of its cost and a lack of rapport with many of the teachers. He enrolled at Wayne State University, although he rarely attended class. He developed a strong relationship with John Egner, a graduate of Yale University who taught painting at Wayne and spoke about art with an authority and rhetorical fervor that made him the philosopher of the Cass Corridor movement.[5] Egner and Newton met when the two had studios in old Convention Hall, a building formerly used for the exhibition of new cars. Newton seemed "like a callow youth when I met him," Egner recalls. "This skinny guy in a T-shirt with jeans. You remember him as being barefoot. Of course, he wasn't, but he always looked that way to you. But Gordon was never the noble savage. He was a real savvy guy who saw things real fast."[6]

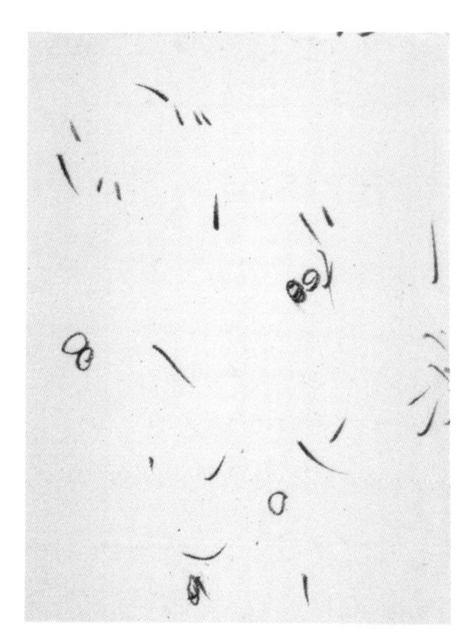

FIGURE 5: **Untitled,** 1972 (Plate 7).

Among Newton's early works are scores of drawings made of squiggles, marks made quickly with a greasy lithographic crayon across a surface, conveying the sense of motion of the artist's arm and body as he worked (see fig. 5). These squiggles and loops are free-floating notations of the speed with which he made them, yet distant enough to seem like specks seen from a satellite. Eventually lines and dashes began appearing, adding gravity and a sense of place. From the vantage point of the roof of his studio building, he had a bird's-eye view of the action on the street, observing, standing on the outside, his preferred position. While Newton wouldn't say whether his abstract marks were a visual equivalent of the people and cars in motion seen from above, the resemblance in these drawings is strong. The marks are certainly not records of exact appearance, but rather form abstract maps, where a person or a car on the street or in a space could be represented by a quick circle of action, in effect creating a new form of cityscape.

During the summer of 1970, Newton did a series of abstract landscapes (see fig. 1) blending dirt with graphite and crayon to produce an atmosphere like that outside an auto plant when the smokestacks are belching and the heat makes the air dark and heavy. Without a horizon line, they are disorienting, as though the viewer is floating in the depicted space, adding another perspective to those the artist was exploring. To move beyond the gesture of the hand, Newton brought his whole body into motion for these works by actually laying on the paper and dragging himself across it, grinding in the dirt. The medium seems to fuse with the paper, not just lying on the surface.

Following these, Newton produced renderings of circles, completely filled in with dense layers of graphite (fig. 6). These big shapes look like the side of a steamroller, all flattened weight and energy. The drawings have a sense of motion, as if they were harnessing or translating the energy used to create them. While they are rather reductive formally, they are intense and direct chronicles of human action and human touch,

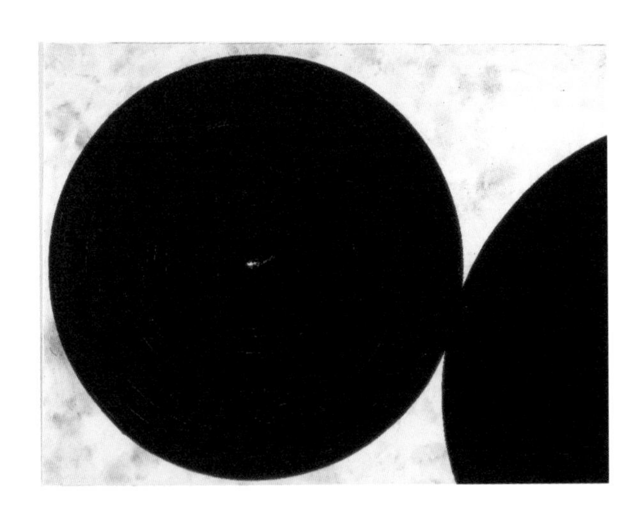

FIGURE 6: **Untitled,** 1974 (Plate 29).

making them immediate, personal, and expressive. Such physicalness is a continual Newton preoccupation.

He also began a series of geometric collages (see fig. 7) that were, perhaps, a counter to the free and expressive landscapes of the summer. This back and forth between the orderly and chaotic in these two series is not an isolated instance, but happens often in the artist's work. More often the two are together in combination in the same piece, particularly in the later works. The dialectic is critical, left at a point of imbalance to impart a sense of impermanence and change. Over the years the structure or organizing device has shifted position in compositions from background to mid-ground to something on the surface over expressionistic layers of abstract imagery. One reads the works in layers, usually from the surface in, rather than as a piece that culminates solely in the surface appearance. Each layer carries its own meanings, allowing Newton to include a depth of information and ideas about a subject that are not bound by place, time, stasis, order, change, or chaos. One layer can be about structure, the other chaos, providing for the paradoxical coexistence of contradictory forces.

One of Newton's earliest supporters was Samuel Wagstaff Jr., curator of modern art at the Detroit Institute of Arts from 1968 to 1971. Wagstaff bought Newton's work for the museum and himself, and encouraged other collectors in town to do the same. In addition, Wagstaff, in his capacity as curator, was able to bring to Detroit contemporary art by the likes of Richard Serra, Robert Smithson, Eva Hesse, Robert Morris, and Michael Heizer, providing local artists a chance to explore and connect with the ideas of others esteemed on a national level. While there is no direct evidence that Newton saw these works or was influenced by them, he does point out, "When you're young, you take in things and change them around, digesting them and coming up with something new... What we were doing was a celebration of life, as simple as that. You had the anti-war, anti-government and authority thing. We were all just making things." When Wagstaff left Detroit for New York in November 1971, he tried to get Newton to move too. But the artist was not interested.

In April 1971 Newton was part of the three-person exhibition marking the opening of the Willis Gallery, a cooperative space begun by the Cass Corridor artists.[7] Newton was always supportive of the Willis. It provided him and the others a consistent and respected exhibition venue, as well as a site for a monthly party. The shows, over the years, included some of the most significant work being done in the area. The openings

FIGURE 7: **Untitled,** 1974 (Plate 25).

were legendary—huge, raucous, sometimes all night celebrations.

Newton and Bob Sestok had a studio downtown in Greektown then. It was cheap, an old industrial space full of litter. The sense of being downtown, which was deserted by late afternoon, in architecturally dominated, silent spaces became a continual subject for Newton's geometry. The trash would become part of his repertoire of materials, as did the ethos of destruction, a constant counter to any construction like the cycles of decaying nature bringing rebirth.

Newton met James F. Duffy Jr. in 1972. Duffy, owner of Edward W. Duffy & Company, a pipe fitting and valve supply company in Detroit, was to become Newton's principal patron, buying drawings, paintings, and three-dimensional pieces regularly. He bought works by Newton and other Detroit artists to place among stacks of pipes in his warehouse, underscoring the correspondence between local art and local industry (see fig. 8). "A lot of what Gordie does I don't understand," Duffy says. "But I spend a lot of time with it I owned many of his heads [of 1989–91] and I spent more time studying them right side up and upside down until I had some sort of idea of what was going on...I've had so many of his works. I'd see them in the morning when I got up and before I went to sleep. Sometimes I'd take my flashlight to see what was going on in the dark. A lot of them can be unattractive on the surface, like his immense series of John Deere tractors. That was an image he worked on. But you've got to get away from the obvious to figure it out."[8]

During the summer of 1972, Newton spent time in northern Michigan, a place to which he would return often. "The environment of Michigan—the pine trees, the Great Lakes, has heavily influenced me, as have the cycles of nature that I see," Newton explained. "I hope to suggest these cycles and the passage or even freezing of time in my work."[9] As the urban landscape outside his Cass Corridor studio infused his art, so too did the surroundings of a northern rural retreat. He brought the two together that summer in one of the first works done upon his return to the city. Daytona Beach consisted of a stack of logs attached to a back board painted with floating geometric shapes. The eight-foot square, imposing structure was part of the exhibition "Twelve Statements: Beyond the 60s" at the Detroit Institute of Arts that September. An exercise in multiple horizons, or horizontals, the work was an odd combination of materials. Newton used the log for what it was—a piece of wood—and also as an erupting element of the painted composition. But the logs couldn't be tamed by paint, remaining displaced, out of sorts, a piece of nature contained, yet uncontrolled.

Daytona Beach was part painting and part relief. The "Figure Eight" works, which followed in 1973, marked the beginning of Newton's long engagement with full-relief sculpture and the constructed object. Moving to three dimensions allowed him to build an interior space and open up his abstract narratives to a kind of physical or actual translation. Having gone as far as he could using his own body to get physical motion into a work, Newton was making a space in which motion—the action he was conveying—could conceivably occur.

The "Figure Eight" sculptures, a translation of a geometric shape Newton had been using in earlier drawings and collages, resembled a racetrack in three-dimensions, with metal and string railings along the edges adding to the sense of speedy movement. "I liked the way it turned around and made a little cycle," said Newton. "It turned on itself. I even thought it would be nice if it made a sound, a sensory sort of thing, so it wouldn't just sit there." The ground of the track was painted all over with inks and resins, creating an abstract image distinct from any meaning attached to the sculptural form itself. This disassociation of materials, shape, and meaning is one of the first instances of Newton layering different ideas and metaphors in his work.

The preoccupation with found and used materials broadened from this point. Newton didn't have the money to buy everything new, essentially requiring that he recycle. But the history that these found objects carried would probably have attracted him anyway. Making such things fit into a work, transforming objects into part of the art while allowing them to keep their prior identity and giving them other identities, was important, permitting him to add more meanings, more related and tangential ideas, more sensual qualities than he could create from scratch.

Newton began using polyester resins as paint in the five horizontal wood molding pieces exhibited at the Willis Gallery in 1973. He applied the resin in coats, taking the works up to the roof to dry. "It reminded me of water," he said of the resins. "It looked real wet and was real strong. It was important stuff. I had reached a point where making marks was not enough. I wanted to go further." Newton painted with the resin, but could also build it into three-dimensional forms, like a rope on a railing. It hardened, yet kept the appearance of a liquid, capturing the actual movement of a liquid running down a surface. In its clear state, layers of resin caught the light, so Newton used it to

FIGURE 8: The Edward W. Duffy & Company Detroit warehouse, where rows of pipes frame a mural by Robert Sestock. (Photograph by Dirk Bakker)

establish tonal values. Instead of painting the effects of light revealing form, he could make this actually occur. As his other materials became more varied and complicated, layers of polyester resin acted as a preservative, holding fragile shapes together and sustaining the whole.

Diamond Follow of 1975 is a large diamond-shaped piece of plywood, covered with canvas, paint, polyester resins, and synthetic fabric. This layered complexity makes the piece a seminal work. First Newton built up rough, but softly colored, valleys and hills on the surface. He then used a jigsaw to slice the outlines of geometric shapes into them, like giant markings in the earth. The surface was worked and reworked until the wrenching cuts of a sawed line met up with a chance splotch of calm, painted color, seemingly leaving no space untouched. Crude, rough, and beautiful in its destruction, the work shows Newton's evolving aesthetic. "I discovered the saw really made some marks. You could make a statement with a tool. You could make your lines. You could work fast. You could almost draw with that thing. I loved using it."

In the following year's Wheel of Fortune (fig. 10), machinery not only shaped the object, but became part of the imagery as well. A huge spiked wheel, reminiscent of an industrial-sized circular saw, juts from the composition's left edge. Part of the wheel has been cut away with a jigsaw. The large circular form is not, however, a piece of industrial equipment, but rather a roulette wheel made of plywood with spokes of leather. An actual ball bearing sits at its center, allowing the

FIGURE 10: **Wheel of Fortune,** 1976, hangs in the Duffy warehouse. (Photograph by Dirk Bakker)

wheel to be spun and giving the piece an interactive quality. The surface of the work is expressively covered with paint and urethanes, which Newton sanded down, leaving gorgeous, runny layers of color. It is an astonishing piece, part kinetic sculpture, part abstract painting, expressive and geometric, referencing a mechanical device and something that could be crafted with it—a blade on the loose, looking as if it could grind itself right off the wall, like an animated device in a cartoon. It could also be seen as an artifact of the industrial culture, a remnant that no longer worked. James Duffy bought it, as well as the earlier Diamond Follow, and set both pieces among the bins of pipe in his warehouse, where they fit right in.

Wheel of Fortune played on the theme of games of chance, a subject with which

Newton had long been fascinated. Chance effects stalked many of the steps he took with his art. Luck wasn't talked about. He played the pinball machines regularly at Cobb's Bar, the neighborhood hangout just down the street from the Willis Gallery. "I don't really understand why I'm so drawn to games," Newton said. "I like the fact that roulette wheels and slot machines are so well made, that the wood is beautifully carved but worn down and that people become so obsessed and involved with them. I would like to think that my work evokes those sorts of associations." [10]

His interest in games connects Wheel of Fortune to the "Roller Coaster" series (fig. 11), which followed in 1977. The roller coaster may be read as a chase or part of a carnival game where one rolls a ball through or down the tracks. The scenario ends with either disaster or success, depending on the rules of the game in play. Essentially the three coasters in the series are about time, a lifetime, narrated from youth to old age. Newton represents time here by using darks and lights, as well as other elements to refer to night and day, birth and death. A sense of the future is suggested by the idea of a car at the start of the roller coaster pointing ahead. A car about to roll down the coaster conveys a sense of motion and the passage of time. Full of shattered illusions, frozen childhood dreams, and joyful play, the coasters may also be read as metaphors for the odyssey of living, with allusions "to movement and stasis, growth and decay, rational order and irrational chaos—all recognizable qualities of human life." [11] In these works, Newton expresses the hope that life's problems can be remedied in order to ride the tracks back up to the end. The coaster "represents life's ups and downs, as well as the fact that you're always moving and traveling during a lifetime," Newton says. "The traumas in your life are indicated by the explosions in the coaster tracks. You've really got to keep your sense of humor." [12]

Newton showed the first two roller coaster pieces locally, at his new Detroit gallery. The Feigenson-Rosenstein Gallery was owned by Jackie Feigenson, previously director of the Willis Gallery, and Judy Rosenstein. Feigenson felt she could do more for the Cass Corridor artists from a commercial gallery space, located in the busy Fisher Building, a short distance away at the northern end of Cass Avenue. Newton saw the move as "a step up to a new gallery right in the neighborhood." The third roller coaster was included in the "Young American Artists: 1978 Exxon

FIGURE 11: **Double Coaster Black and White,** 1977, 18 x 82 x 7 7/8 in., wood, oil paint, and wax. Founders Society Purchase, Dr. and Mrs. George Kamperman Fund (F77.90).

National Exhibition," at the Solomon R. Guggenheim Museum in New York and purchased for that museum's collection.

Newton's next projects, "Diving Boards" and "Cast Cement" drawings and structures, appear more architecturally inspired, geometric, and highly ordered than the roller coasters. He created "Diving Boards;" towers of glass boards balanced on glass or plasticene blocks and dripping with polyester resin, after a summer spent in a cabin near Lake Superior. Newton was using both the glass and resin to create a sense of water and of light on the water. The fragility of the materials and the askew arrangement of the boards bring to mind questions about jumping into the unknown. There is a sense of fear conveyed by these small objects consisting of boards paralyzed in random positions by resin. By the end of the series, the glass panels formed the walls of more architectural spaces, and the pieces were burned, charred like an abandoned building on a city street.

FIGURE 12: **Cast Cement,** 1979 (Plate 45).

The architectural drawings and structures of "Cast Cement" are colder (see fig. 12). Done at the request of then director of the Detroit Institute of Arts, Frederick Cummings, they are plans for a proposed sculpture garden outside the museum. Cummings told Newton to make it an indestructible plaza, so he imagined it made out of cast cement. Newton made a few models out of wood, painted gray. They looked more like a maze made out of toy blocks, the extreme of an urban space as mannerist bunker, not a garden for art. "I think I could cast anything of cement and put it together," he said. "I have all these fresh ideas."

During the next decade, Newton continued using the materials, vocabulary, and working methods he had developed in the 1970s, voraciously exploring new ideas. The underwater life of Lake Huron inspired his "Marine Shelf" drawings (see fig. 13). This series served as a means for Newton to work out ideas for a huge construction (28 by 120 by 24 inches) containing many platforms and beams, broken and barely passable like the decks of an oil rig or the remnants of some Atlantis-like city. "It was an underwater city. It kept growing and becoming the ruins of a civilization." The entire structure is covered in polyester resin, with clearer resin dripping from ends and darkened resin near the middle. Using darks and lights, Newton imparts the piercing quality of light penetrating underwater. The piece became increasingly ambitious and complex as Newton worked on it in his garage from 1982 to 1985. When it got too big and kept breaking, he revised it,

FIGURE 13: **Untitled (Marine Shelf),** 1980 (Plate 57).

a common practice. He had no problem with remaking something two or three years after he first completed it, if he felt it needed rethinking.

An exhibition in April 1983 at the Feigenson Gallery, "Structo-Vision," featured fantastic inventions—part book, part sculpture, part painting—depicting pickup trucks as an emblem of American farmlands. Newton had spent time on a farm as a child and that life was compelling to him. He always drove pickups, which he adapted, restored, and painted, until they looked like offshoots of his art.

A printed manifesto, written by the artist but left unsigned, "Structo-Vision: Setting Forth an Introductory Theorem of Structurally Integral, Visual Phenomena, Drawing Deeply from the Reservoir of Subconscious Human Imagery," was distributed at the show. A mystery, at first the theory expounded is difficult to follow, like some art talk–psychobabble: "In nature, STRUCTO-VISION is a stimulus," the last paragraph said, "triggered by a physically inherent visual factor, a pre-conceived, integral rationalization of how something is seen. The depth of this realization is felt suddenly. This recurring phenomenon may reach such a high level of physical absorption that a sense of visual disorientation takes place, leaving one with deep biological repercussions, which do—in time—become growing neurological necessities."[13] The words serve as an introduction to the world conjured in the art. The written tract provides a sense that its author believes there is a scientific explanation, emanating from human biology, for certain visual responses.

Each work in "Structo-Vision" consisted of a series of canvas pages hung from a wooden rack attached to the wall, like an instruction manual in some machine shop. Elaborate constructions perched on a shelf above the canvases looked like a sound system or two-way radio built up to a point where the objects seem out of control. Stuffed animals and pottery, homey reminders of life on a farm, were also set on the shelves. The paintings themselves were an imaginative dissection of a red pickup, with each page detailing a different aspect of the vehicle. The first page depicted a truck squealing off into space—wheels flying, dirt marked with tire tracks expanding into gigantic proportions. Next came the mechanical and tool diagrams, invented but with seeming connections to the vehicles' owner's manuals. Other canvases examined the relation of such trucks to popular culture—the clubs, the races, the social life. Finally, the last pages contained canvas cutouts in the shape of circuit boards, looking like the diodes and silicon chips that power computers. Newton was constructing a virtual world where tools, games, remnants, words, and images recalled farm life—a type of place, a lifestyle, and the people who lived it.

While working on these assemblages, Newton also became interested in the technology of spying. An avid reader, he was immersed in spy novels at the time. He was bothered by the proliferation of surveillance devices, including tape recorders and cameras on streets and in stores monitoring daily activities. With the six-foot-tall construction SDX Satellite Delay (fig. 14), he built a facsimile of a communications apparatus that appears threatening. A robot-like wooden monolith containing precisely crafted fronts of video cameras, stereo equipment, tape decks and computers, the sculpture distilled, reconstructed, and commented on the power of technology.

FIGURE 14: **SDX Satellite Delay,** 1983–84, 76 x 41 x 30 in., wood, iron, styrofoam, rubber, varnish, and oil paint. Gift of Mr. and Mrs. S. Brooks Barron (1988.24).

Newton collects toy trucks, tractors, and robots. Wherever he lived over the years, he would display his collections on a wall of shelves. The toys, as facsimiles of the real thing, were important models for his renderings. They are also reminders, remnants of childhood. Oliver Twist, from 1988, a huge, amazing construction inspired by Charles Dickens's book, seems to come the closest to dealing with the subject of youth. The Dickens book is, in part, about the lost security of childhood. Newton, who had English ancestors, was contemplating his past at this time. The construction, which he said was his most complex, is so layered with objects that it is difficult to decode. A section of the assemblage, which sticks out from the wall, consists of wooden cutouts of keys in many variations, dangling about like a giant shop sign. Some are burnt a crusty black. Wooden shelves against the wall display used stuffed animals, dolls, and other things Newton made. The piece has a darkness, as though it is lodged deep in memory, in history, in a place one has never visited or perhaps doesn't want to visit.

In 1989, Newton left the Feigenson Gallery, moving to the Susanne Hilberry Gallery in Birmingham. That year Hilberry showed a group of sixty-eight paintings on paper of torsos and heads, titled "Love, Life, Geometric Heritage," a project Newton continued to add to for many years. "Marine Studies," a series of relief constructions about boats that evolved from his earlier "Marine Shelf" project, appeared at the Joy Emery Gallery in Grosse Pointe at the same time.

American agriculture was the subject of a series Newton worked on from the early 1980s to 1991, dedicated to images of tractors. While living in Kansas as a boy, he drove tractors and seemed to have developed a deep respect for them. He began collecting old

John Deere models, joined a tractor club, and subscribed to a collector's magazine, completely immersing himself in the farm culture. The tractors brought to mind rural landscapes, and Newton was interested in some of the art depicting these places. He even sent Hilberry a postcard of a George Luks rolling mountain landscape, Roundhouses at Highbridge (1909–1910), writing the words "Agriculture is an Abstraction. Yes Indeed," on the back. "The history of this country and how serious we are about preserving that history relates to agriculture," he says.

For Newton, who cares about machine tools, grows his own food whenever possible, and studies nature, farming and its implements are important subjects. He made his tractors in a variety of formats, as realistic pictures, cartoon diagrams, and abstracted images (see fig. 15). Some were cut out of cardboard and wood. An admirer of the way J. M. W. Turner painted light, Newton dedicated a group of these pictures to that nineteenth-century British master. Newton's light is darker and conveyed in strong brush strokes, which give the feeling of a storm pressing in. While the tractor is part of the male culture, both as a childhood toy and adult tool, there is a further meaning. The tractor becomes a metaphor for the artist, riding this machine on a field, alone, and making marks in the earth.

After he made the tractor drawings, Newton began to scale back exhibitions of his work, but he continued making art. He had less connection to many of the area's artists, keeping in contact with only a few people, including Jim Duffy. Their relationship was respectfully close, yet a bit cantankerous, with Newton supplying an edge and unpredictability to Duffy's very organized life.

Newton recently moved into a beautiful, old Arts and Crafts–style home near the Detroit River, saying he has always liked the city through all these years. Wherever he lives, Newton rebuilds his world around him. He subscribes to magazines, trade journals, and catalogs covering a vast range of subjects from the mundane to the art related and scientific. Once the publications are read, or absorbed, pieces of them turn up in collages or as paper for the paintings he still does by the hundreds. The density of information in this age of global communication has become one of his subjects.

FIGURE 15: **Untitled (Agriculture)**, 1992, (Plate 70).

During the 1990s, he created three extraordinary boxes, one of which he exhibited at the Hilberry Gallery. Thick black frames hold layers of glass, with each layer laden with resin. Rather than containing a picture, an image, or an object, the frames seem to hold a fog so dense it creates a blur, which prevents the viewer from focusing on anything specific. As mysterious as anything Newton has done, the pieces capture the unknown. They force one to look inward, to wonder what isn't seen.

Newton's thoughts returned to his Cass Corridor days in the fall of 2000, when he did a painting in memory of fellow artist Ann Mikolowski, who had recently died. Newton was a close friend of both Mikolowski and her husband Ken, a poet. In 1969, the couple founded and ran the Alternative Press in the basement of a building on Cass Avenue. The press published postcards, banners, and broadsides by artists and poets of the period. The Mikolowskis were like family to most of the Corridor artists. Newton spent a lot of time at their kitchen table, making art for the press. Newton remembered Mikolowski and painted a small work for her. The surface of the painting is the deepest cobalt from edge to edge. The dark blue covers layers and layers of hidden colors, expressive marks, and unknown images, building to the surface with a reservoir of memories, time elapsed, and experiences past that can only be sensed. He has buried all that was under a celestial shroud.

More than thirty years have passed since Gordon Newton moved to Detroit, the Cass Corridor, and the small, intense art world contained there. His art is still about taking a form or image and changing it over and over again to explore many possibilities. While connections to his personal life are buried in his work, so are his interpretations of significant events in the larger culture, together forming a chronicle of the last three decades. His passage from the free experimentation of his youth to his current state of introspection has been a natural one. He doesn't leave the past behind but carries it forward as one more layer submerged in the density of his art.

For Newton, his art is all consuming. After thirty years, it doesn't seem to matter who sees what he has done or who acknowledges what he has done. He will still do it.

NOTES

1. Gordon Newton, interviews by author, April-May 2001. All quotes from Gordon Newton, unless otherwise noted, are derived from these interviews.

2. Earl Robinette, interview by author, April 2001.

3. The artists working in this style included Newton, William Antonow, James Chatelain, John Egner, Steven Foust, Douglas James, Michael Luchs, Nancy Mitchnick, Ellen Phelan, Nancy Pletos, Paul Schwarz, and Robert Sestok. Newton was closest to Sestok. The two met at the Arts and Crafts school, where Sestok was a studio assistant in charge of firing the kilns. Newton was and continues to be interested in ceramics, making pieces from time to time. He and Sestok shared studios and apartments in their early years as artists.

4. Mary Jane Jacob, "Kick Out the Jams: The Emergence of a Detroit Avant-Garde," in Kick Out the Jams: Detroit's Cass Corridor, 1963–1977 (The Detroit Institute of Arts, exh. cat., 1980), 31.

5. Newton feels that Egner's intelligent commentary was a major reason for the seriousness of the local art scene. Artists were stimulated to work up to Egner's critical level. Newton describes Egner's role: "He could communicate between the artists and public. He was the interpreter. He was always supporting everyone."

6. John Barron, "Newton's Universe," Detroit Monthly (March 1988): 90.

7. Greg Murphy, a poet and artist, found the space at 422 W. Willis in the Cass Corridor and arranged for the thirty-dollar-a-month rent. Other artists, including Aris Koutroulis and Nancy Mitchnick, organized the space.

8. James F. Duffy Jr., interview by author, April 2001.

9. Quoted in Jay Belloli, "New Faces/New Images," Ocular Magazine 4,4 (winter 1979): 38.

10. Linda Shearer, Young American Artists, 1978 Exxon National Exhibition (New York: Solomon R. Guggenheim Museum, exh. cat., 1978), 50.

11. Ruth Rattner, "Gordon Newton," Bulletin of the Detroit Institute of Arts 58, 2 (1980): 92.

12. Shearer (note 10), 50.

13. Structo-Vision (Detroit: Feigenson Gallery, April 1983).

LINE, SHAPE, FORM
THREE DECADES OF DRAWINGS

MARYANN WILKINSON

FIGURE 16: **Untitled (Family Tree),** 1981 (Plate 75).

LINE, SHAPE, FORM: THREE DECADES OF DRAWINGS

IT MEANS SOMETHING BUT YOU
CAN'T FIND THE WORDS FOR IT.

— GORDON NEWTON

LINE, SHAPE, FORM: THREE DECADES OF DRAWINGS

For Gordon Newton, making art is "all about solving problems."[1] He is probably best known for his ambitious sculpture, enigmatic assemblages of found and transformed objects. "Gordon Newton: Selections from the James F. Duffy Jr. Gift," an exhibition of three decades of his works on paper, presents an aspect of his oeuvre that is perhaps less familiar than the sculpture but reveals more of his thinking about art. Newton's work is serious, systematic, and deliberate, exploring a wide range of subject matter and interests. He refers to all of his work done on or with paper as "drawings." Working in series, often developing several different ones concurrently, Newton found that drawings, unlike sculpture, gave him the freedom to work quickly and in multiples as a means of teasing out ideas or forms that intrigued him.

The earliest work in this exhibition dates from about 1970, the time when Newton took a studio in what was known as Convention Hall, a former new car exhibition space on Cass Avenue. It was there that many of the artists known as the "Cass Corridor" group lived and worked together. By 1970, Newton had abandoned an earlier illustrative style and was working in a much more spare, rapid, abstract mode. With strong, assured strokes of lithographic crayon or graphite sticks on white paper, he tried to emphasize the surface of the paper by the application of linear and circular elements (see fig. 17). He made dozens of these drawings, varying the sizes of paper and the complexity of design. Essentially black and white, some of the works also incorporate areas of delicate color. The drawings have been described elsewhere as having a relationship to the view of freeways, streets, and cars outside his window or as a way to visualize landscape patterns, as if gathering inspiration from photographs of the Earth from outer space.[2] His interest in mapping suggested by these works is more clearly visible in studies for a lithography project of this period done directly onto commercially printed maps. In retrospect, Newton suggests that the link between individual pieces and specific imagery is tenuous, referring to this group in general as "energy" drawings: "[I] didn't really have time to make an image. There were so many high energy people working all around [me] that they were just a way to capture that energy." While the drawings capture the speed and spontaneity of their creation, they are highly controlled, tautly structured, and represent a sophisticated shift into abstraction by the

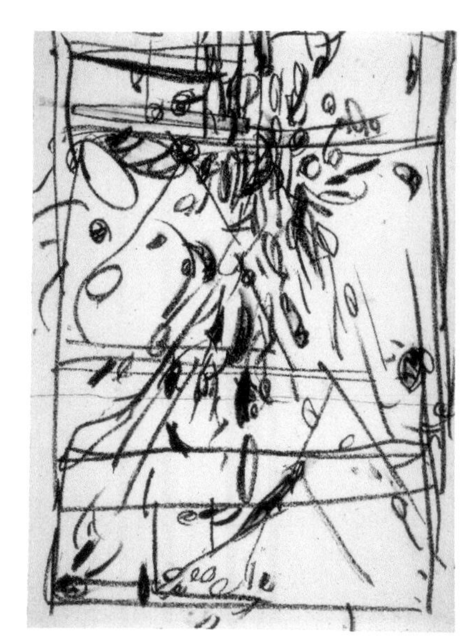

FIGURE 17: **Untitled,** 1971 (Plate 4).

then twenty-two-year-old Newton. Eventually, they took on a more intuitive, looser, less gridlike approach to the application of geometric forms. With an elegance and rhythm reminiscent of Kandinsky, the sensitivity and freedom of these works is an interesting contrast to the highly controlled drawings Newton was doing simultaneously.

In these contemporaneous, more strictly geometric works, areas of velvety matte black coalesce into hard-edged, interlocking polygons, balanced by the white or buff paper left as a negative space. Narrow strips of clear cellophane or opaque white tape stand in for the drawn line in some of these drawings, creating even sharper definitions between areas of the composition (see fig. 18). Over time, the cellophane has yellowed, adding an unanticipated element of color to the works and enhancing their linear properties. The tape now has a presence defined not only by edge and shiny surface but also by the yellowing of age, an effect prized by Newton in his later work.

FIGURE 18: **Untitled,** 1972 (Plate 15).

The inclusion of the tape signals the beginning of Newton's work with collage and the expansion of the concept of mark making to include more than a handheld stylus. The idea of aerial perspective merges with his interest in architectural plans, suggested by these interlocking and rational forms. The lines of narrow cellophane and white tape stand in for some of the dark graphite lines used in the previous series, imposing a negative/positive approach to imagery. The tape disturbs the flatness of the paper, building out almost imperceptibly from the surface as a counter to the traditional notion of depth behind the picture plane. At the same time, however, Newton developed the convention of outlining the edges of the paper in black, insisting on the limits and boundaries of the paper and reasserting the flatness of the surface.

A third series, large-scale landscapes, was developed at the same time (see fig. 1). These works are astonishingly beautiful in their emphasis on accident and a roughly worked surface, entirely opposite in feeling to the geometric series. Newton speaks of these landscapes as having been inspired by the look and color of nature, particularly by the dense brown-grays of the underbrush and soil in northern Michigan. These landscapes do not bear the same evidence of control as do the other series; instead, the medium is physically worked into the paper, rubbed and scrubbed, even scuffed with the artist's shoes to scumble and grind the surface. Holes worn into the paper are backed with pigmented tape or strips of paper, and underpainting in soft colors is imperfectly covered over with a broad brush and strokes of dark paint. Fingerprints and pencil scribbles add to the work's texture, density, and untamed quality. An organizing sense of structure is only suggested by the straight line of black electrician's tape that runs across the bottom, halted abruptly on the right by a messy, globular foldover of tape, heavy with paint. In other areas, precisely trimmed squares of tape provide a visual stop to anchor the shifting surfaces. The contrast in formal approach of the geometric works and the landscape drawings establishes a pattern that characterizes Newton's artistic production. Never content to work in a single medium or idiom, he continually expands and refines his sense of his own style.

Newton's work from 1974, as represented in the James F. Duffy Jr. gift, moves from the abstract to the figurative and back again in each of three accomplished groups of works: the "Constructions"; the "Record Album" drawings; and the "Fuselage" drawings.[3] Each series has a figurative basis, which the artist sometimes makes abstract and sometimes does not. In the early months of that year, Newton moved a step beyond his earlier geometric compositions to create paper collage "constructions" that push into three-dimensions. He remarked later that the earlier works "looked like they wanted to be cut up and now they are." The first of these constructions grew out of Newton's cutting sheets of paper and putting shapes together. Newton was careful to maintain a personal scale, small enough so that "a person can pick it up and look at it." The works within the series incorporate painted and commercially colored paper, plastic screening, and masking tape, all chosen for their formal qualities including color, texture, and pattern. As in the earlier series, tape is used as a linear element, but here it also is a quick way to adhere the separate shapes. Similarly, the inclusion of lined notebook paper might function as an easy substitute for the hand-drawn parallel lines on other segments of the same work or others in the series. Here, line is used as form, to describe a shape as well as to define an edge or to suggest volume or mass. While an important investigation of formal principles, these works nonetheless have a connection to the physical properties of the natural world. Inscriptions on the back of some of them, such as "February Daylight: Snowed In," suggest that the linear forms and pale tones have a relationship to the weak, slanting light of mid-winter in Michigan. Newton's interest in the effects of light and its ability to dissolve or distort physical appearances, hinted at in this early series, will assume greater prominence in his work of the next decade.

FIGURE 19: **Untitled,** 1974 (Plate 28).

The "Record Album" works from the same year take a different formal approach to drawing. Obsessive and energetic circles of heavy graphite, done with a graphite stick attached to a string, create a simple but formal composition (see fig. 19). The shapes are rigidly controlled and perfect, with sections of circles that just graze the edge of the others. By contrast, the smudging in the white areas plays with the notion of fingerprints used so prominently in other works and contradicts the formality of the graphite circles. In one work, a partial disk is created the same way, with the hard and unnuanced tip of a ballpoint pen. A sculpture that echoes this aesthetic embeds a real record album into a sheet of Plexiglas. The Plexiglas was then raggedly cut with a saw, and its surface roughened in a mimicry of the painted gesture of brush and stylus. The record retains its perfect shape, nearly obliterated by the chaos around it. Another sculpture turns the disks into Plexiglas circles of graduated sizes and stands them on end as a group in a plaster landscape. The use of the record album seems to make visible for the first time the notion of sound in Newton's visual pieces, a relationship that would figure prominently in his future work: "I always like the idea that you could look at a drawing and hear it, hear music or something."

The circular motifs and the interest in sound also play a part in the "Figure Eight" drawings done at about the same time. For Newton, the figure eight takes on a repetitive, obsessive, turned-back-on-itself quality that is similar in concept to the graphite disks. Linear and solid at the same time, the shape implies momentum or a never-ending, effortless movement. He refers to the figure eight as a shape without beginning or end, constantly reinventing itself as the same form. The "Roller Coaster" series of 1977 combines this sense of perpetual motion with an architectural structure. In other works, the shape mutates into reel-to-reel audio and videotapes. The "Fuselage" group is a surprising and beautiful set of drawings from the summer of 1974 (see fig. 20). These drawings are based on the upright tail of an airplane, but this recognizable image is overlaid with abstract and geometric forms, perhaps suggesting the mechanics and physics of flight: radar screens, flight patterns, aerial maps. The fuselage, in reality a rounded, tubular shape, is rendered relatively flat in the drawings. In the artist's mind, however, it retains that curvilinear character and sense of motion, even though the viewer can make that inference only by knowing the shape of the body of an actual plane. In these complex and exciting drawings, Newton reveals his ability to create a composition of many disparate parts that yet manages to work together as a whole, leading the viewer's eye across the sheet to explore individual areas. The choice of the paper—with either a hard finish or soft one—changes the character of the imagery from cool to warm, as does his choice of materials, which range from graphite to ballpoint pen to collage. Of particular interest is his

FIGURE 20: **Untitled (Fuselage)**, 1974 (Plate 32).

distinctive use of collage in these works. Here, a square of paper is collaged onto an area of the paper support as a way of reinforcing its flatness; Newton likes its literal presence as a contrast to the virtual volume of the fuselage imagery.

FIGURE 21: **Siren,** 1979 (Plate 46).

Like many of Newton's series, the "Fuselage" group is composed of many drawings of the same subject done in a short span of time —months, weeks, or even days—and then abandoned. By the end of the 1970s, however, two important subjects, architectural-based drawings and those arising from the natural world, entered his work and would remain as themes and imagery over the subsequent twenty years. The architectural series "Cast Cement" began as a proposal for an outdoor sculpture on the southwest lawn of the Detroit Institute of Arts, where then director Frederick J. Cummings was considering building a sculpture garden. Newton's project, done in many elevations and a few three-dimensional models, was a proposal for an open architectural setting of large rectangular slabs of concrete (see fig. 21). His notion was of a sculpture that could be used as seating and as a picnic area, one that would be "indestructible." Its cool, intellectual expression of space, playing off his interest in architecture and building, became, with the addition of running figures and explosive devices, a quasi-narrative of urban unrest. The flattened, sticklike figures were inserted into the drawings to lend a sense of scale, Newton says. The details added to the outdoor sculpture make it look more like a cityscape. Fireworks or some other kind of explosives also punctuate and add color to these works; inscriptions on the back such as "Siren" make narrative allusions.

Linked to this series is a group of drawings and models of cabins and workshops, perhaps done as an antidote to or a refuge from the pressures of city life. "Holiday Cabin," a wooden building in a natural setting with large exploding firecrackers on each side, seems the flip side of "Siren." The three-dimensional models (see fig. 22) suggest a more directed ordering of environment than the cabin drawings. Meticulously detailed down to windowpanes and sawdust on the

FIGURE 22: **Model of a Carpenter's Workshop,** 1976, 8 5/8 x 8 3/4 in., wood, glass, paint, paper, varnish, steel, and cotton. Gift of James F. Duffy Jr. (1999.1520).

floor, these structures are the clearest statement of his love of architecture and his interest in visualizing and planning living spaces.

Those interests were given free rein in the series "On the Thames, English Cottage," which he began around 1984 and continued into the mid-1990s (see fig. 23). Reading about the lives of English artists inspired Newton to create this series, a fantasy architectural project for a London house. In a group of floor plan drawings, Newton carefully works out every element of the setting, from the central woodburning stove, which anchors the house, to the pathway past the garden and pool to the river. In contrast to the mid-1970s abstractions that seem compartmentalized and constructed like floor plans or the cool rigor of "Cast Cement," these works are suffused with brilliant color and detail. A key to the artist's thinking can be found on the back of each of the two largest and most comprehensive plan drawings from 1992. On each, a photograph cut from a magazine has been glued to the sheet and annotated. On one drawing is an aerial view of Innes House, a mansion in the English countryside, complete with formal gardens and pathways; on the other, a photo of the empty site where the new British Library was about to be built. Like other imaginary architectural projects he has envisaged, this one favors an aerial perspective and contrasts exterior geometry with an intuitive interior. The large number of these works, spread out over a number of years, suggests Newton's fascination with this idea, both formally and conceptually.

FIGURE 23: **Untitled (On the Thames, English Cottage),** 1991 (Plate 119)

FIGURE 24: **Untitled,** 1981 (Plate 54).

At the same time, Newton worked on a group of drawings that looked at the natural world as both abstraction and structure. The "Marine Shelf" series of 1981 took as its subject underwater plant life. Groups of long-stemmed, exotic plants rendered in strong colors seem to be transformed into machinery or bridge spans (see fig. 24). The imagery maintains an uneasy tension between the natural and the artificial, seeming to shift back and forth between delicate, waving plants and hard-edged gigantic rigging. The relationship or transformation of the natural world to that of the one fabricated by humans and then back again is at the core of much of Newton's work. The roller coasters, for example, are highly engineered structures, which in Newton's hands become melting, dripping shapes in the sculptures (see fig. 11) or the curly shape of a sea creature in the drawings (cover, plates 30 and 31).

Newton also considered human beings as part of a structure or process. The "Anthology" series of 1981 consists of a dozen small works of graphite on paper (see fig. 25). Their structure is based on blueprint-type plans, sometimes with cutout collaged elements that have a formal relationship to the "English Cottage" and "Roller Coaster" imagery. Newton covered the entire surface of the paper, including the collage elements, with a dense, shiny coating of graphite, used in a way not seen since the "Record Album" drawings of 1974. He has identified the underlying linear structure of these works as representative of the organization of a genealogy chart. This links "Anthology" directly to the exquisite "Family Tree" series done concurrently (see fig. 16). In the latter series, the upright forms of the "Marine Shelf" plants seem to be inverted and simplified, hanging from the top down like a vertical bar graph. Their formal structure and delicate waxy surface is meant to evoke all of the artist's concerns, from architecture to plant life to the structure of families, each for Newton a dynamic, linear development.

FIGURE 25: **Untitled (Anthology)**, 1981 (Plate 60).

FIGURE 26: **Untitled (Warfare)**, 1982 (Plate 79).

"Agriculture" (1991–92) and "Warfare" (1993) push his ideas about structure as process and an individual's relationship with the natural world in slightly different directions (figs. 15 and 26). The two series explore machinery and its use in shaping modern life, but they do so with almost completely opposite points of view. "Agriculture" concentrates on farmers riding tractors, sometimes in a farmyard setting, and presents a benign, harmonious view of the interrelationship of human beings and machine. By contrast, in "Warfare" the machine is not visibly controlled by a person but rather appears as a self-propelled instrument of destruction.

Newton developed a long-standing interest in agriculture, spending time in rural areas, subscribing to farming magazines, and joining farmers' organizations. Fascinated by its seasonal rhythms, he describes farming as "so abstract," a world with its own language, codes, rituals, and culture. He recalls, "I thought it would be fun to treat it seriously," and began a group of works dealing specifically with the tractor. Some of the most interesting works of this group, which includes collages, drawings, and low-relief sculpture made of foam core, isolate the tractor engine as the subject. Meticulously detailed, even to specific model years, these drawn engines are covered over with a layer of varnish, a technique Newton first used in the "Marine Light" studies of the mid-1980s. The varnish's effect on the paper lends a contrasting pattern to the drawn shapes as well as infusing the composition with soft, flickering light. The dark palette and the thick varnish of the "Warfare" drawings, with their images of rolling tanks, creates an atmosphere of silent menace. Television coverage of conflict in the Middle East prompted Newton to make these drawings, but he has expressed dismay at the stark violence of the images.

FIGURE 27: **Untitled,** 1989 (Plate 94).

The use of varnish to coat the surface of his works on paper has become a signature aspect of Newton's style. He found its greatest use in his dynamic series of heads, begun in 1988 (see fig. 27). Newton says he was interested in working in a figurative style "because no one else was" and chose, for the first time in his career, the human form as subject. Focusing on the head and neck, he abstracted the figures to circles and cylinders, painted in heavy outline or built up through collage. Newton then added more oil stick, paint, additional collage, and wood stain or varnish, which soaked into the paper like watercolor, remaining flexible to the touch. Finally, he applied layer upon layer of varnish, "to seal it all up so it would last for a long time." Intimate yet intimidating, the heads provide a simple geometric framework onto which Newton can hang his heavily worked surfaces, rich with emotional and personal connotations.

The "Heads" series was initially inspired by the 1988 Olympic Games in Seoul when Newton was struck by the sheer physical power of the athletes and the degree of strength, discipline, and perfection required of them beyond that of ordinary people. But when seen in a television interview from the neck up, these superhumans suddenly resumed their vulnerability. Painted on a human scale, the earliest heads project an image of self-determination and power with which the viewer can identify; as the series evolved, the character of the images changed dramatically. The first heads have legible facial features, which in later drawings mutate, become distorted, and finally disappear almost completely. The ears on some of the heads, often the only recognizable feature remaining, grow large as if over-functioning and are sometimes applied as collage. The emphasis on the ears reintroduces Newton's interest in sound, or the act of hearing. A group of heads from around 1990 were inspired by the eighteenth-century "Toby" jugs and their characteristically distorted faces, distinctive colors, and shiny glazing. A few of these are inscribed on the back "carbon procedure," a reference to the dating and reinterpretation by archaeologists of something old that has been rediscovered. "Everything old looks so good," Newton remarked in reference to the "Toby" heads.

Throughout the "Heads" series, the brushstrokes are broad and slashing; the paint handling and the heavy use of black lend a sense of violence and fear to the works. The varnish coating is used in these pictures not to suggest the presence of light, but rather to underscore the immutability of each image. In some works, the varnish is allowed to drip down to the bottom and over the edge of the paper, clearly delineating the end of the sheet but also leaving the uncomfortable impression of something—perhaps the features?—melting and sliding off the page. The relationship between the imagery and the medium has an evocative power that goes well beyond the rest of Newton's work. As the features of the head become increasingly obliterated, the prospect of looking directly inside the skull seems possible, as if some important truth about human beings is there to be seen. While it may be tempting to read the heads as portraits or even self-portraits, they instead emphasize the questions the artist is asking about the nature of the self.

From the early abstract drawings to the evocative power of the heads, Gordon Newton's works over the last thirty years are never entirely what they appear to be. He hopes that the works are only the starting point for the mind to wander into far-off places: "It means something but you can't find the words for it." Ideas of structure, nature, and, most of all, change inform his work—but it is a change that doubles back on itself like a figure eight, with a sense of perpetual motion. This generous gift to the Detroit Institute of Arts made by James F. Duffy Jr. allows for the careful study of the "problem solving" of this protean artist, who weaves together, with logic tempered by emotion, a vision of contemporary life.

NOTES

I am grateful to Gordon Newton for discussing his work and ideas with me. In addition, I would like to thank my collaborator on this exhibition, Nancy Sojka, for the many insightful and interesting ideas she has brought to my understanding of this work. This essay is based in part on "Gordon Newton: Life, Love, and the Geometric Heritage," in Gordon Newton, published by the Joy Emery Gallery and the Susanne Hilberry Gallery, 1989.

1. All quotes from the artist are from a series of interviews with the author, held between March 21 and April 21, 2001.

2. Ruth Rattner, "Gordon Newton," Bulletin of the Detroit Institute of Arts 58, 2 (1979): 83-84.

3. At the artist's request, works are referred to by their series titles only. He calls the words on the back of individual drawings "inscriptions."

The Duffy Gift

In 1999, Detroit-area collector James F. Duffy Jr. gave the Detroit Institute of Arts a vast collection of works on paper by Gordon Newton. This gift included over five hundred drawings, forty sketchbooks and/or sketchpads, two paintings, twelve pieces of sculpture, and folder after folder of archival materials related to the works of art and the artist.

The current exhibition of approximately 150 drawings was selected from this larger body of work and represents the principal themes and subjects that have occupied Newton's attention since the 1970s. Several of these themes or series constitute a majority of the entire collection. They are the "Heads," "On the Thames," "Agriculture," "Marine Shelf" project, "Cast Cement" project, "Geometric Constructions," and the simple graphite and crayon drawings of the early 1970s. The drawings range from scores of finished compositions similar to those in the exhibition to hundreds of more schematic studies.

The pages of the sketchbooks, sketchpads, and many pads of ledger paper are filled with quick, rough ideas related to these same themes. If each sheet of paper is counted separately, the Duffy gift totals several thousand drawings. Most of the drawings were executed in the same mediums illustrated in this catalogue. However, many of the sketches in the ledger pads were made with colored ink markers and a variety of felt tipped pens. When combined with the larger, finished drawings of the same subject, these sketches demonstrate the serious thought and considerable effort Newton devoted to each series.

Among the subjects not represented in the exhibition are several small groups of figurative scenes. These depict golfers on the putting green; robot-like creatures; a robust, muscular figure; and a small number of images of an arm and fist related to a sculpture for another local collector, Florence Barron. Another very small series is devoted to studies of chairs.

The Duffy gift of drawings joins twenty-one other works by Gordon Newton given to the museum by various donors in previous years.

NANCY SOJKA

PLATES

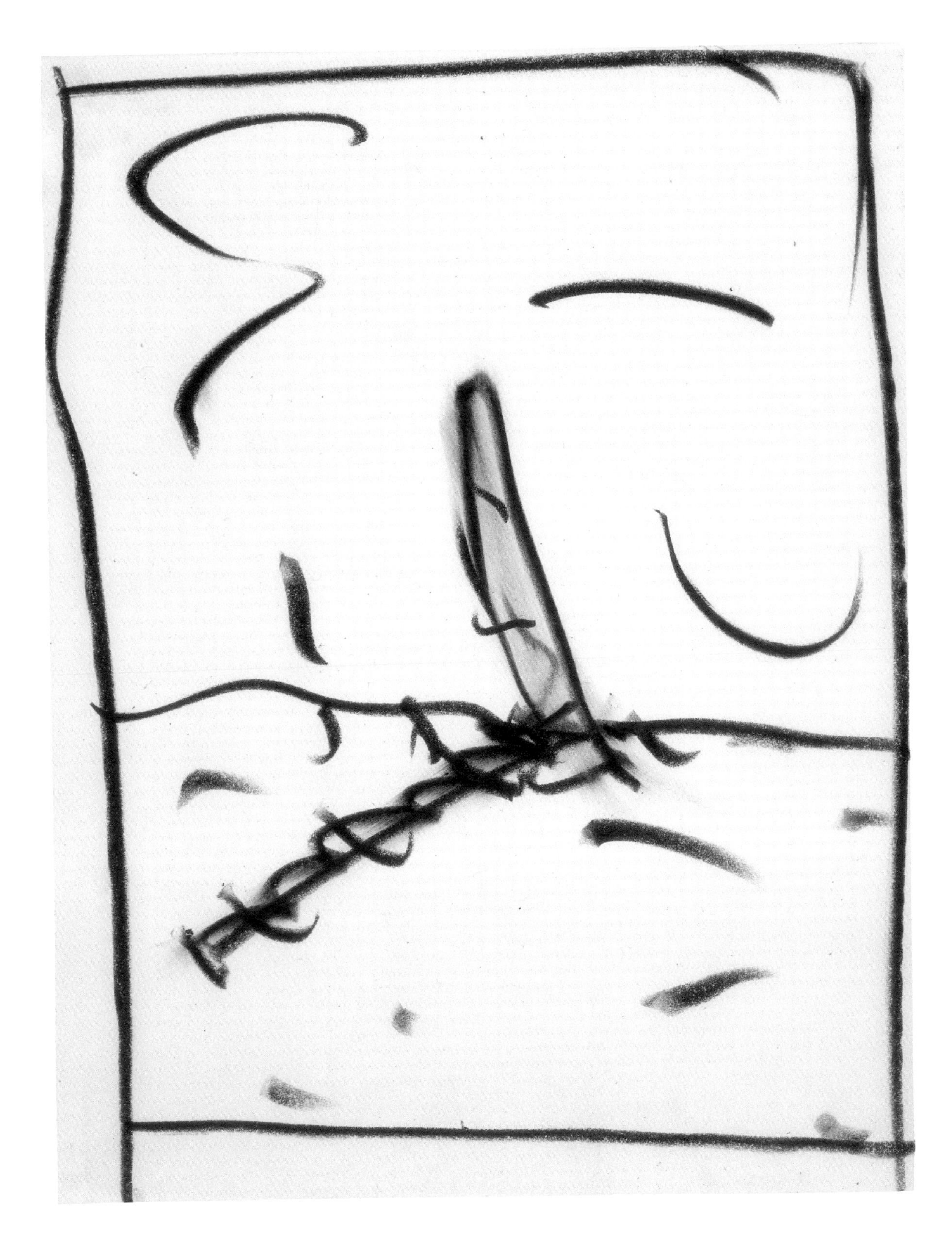

Untitled, 1970

11 x 8⅜ in.

Crayon

1999.403

PLATE 1

PLATE 2

Untitled, 1971
17 x 14 in.
Crayon and paint
1999.1365

Untitled, 1971
24 x 18 in.
Crayon
1999.241

PLATE 3

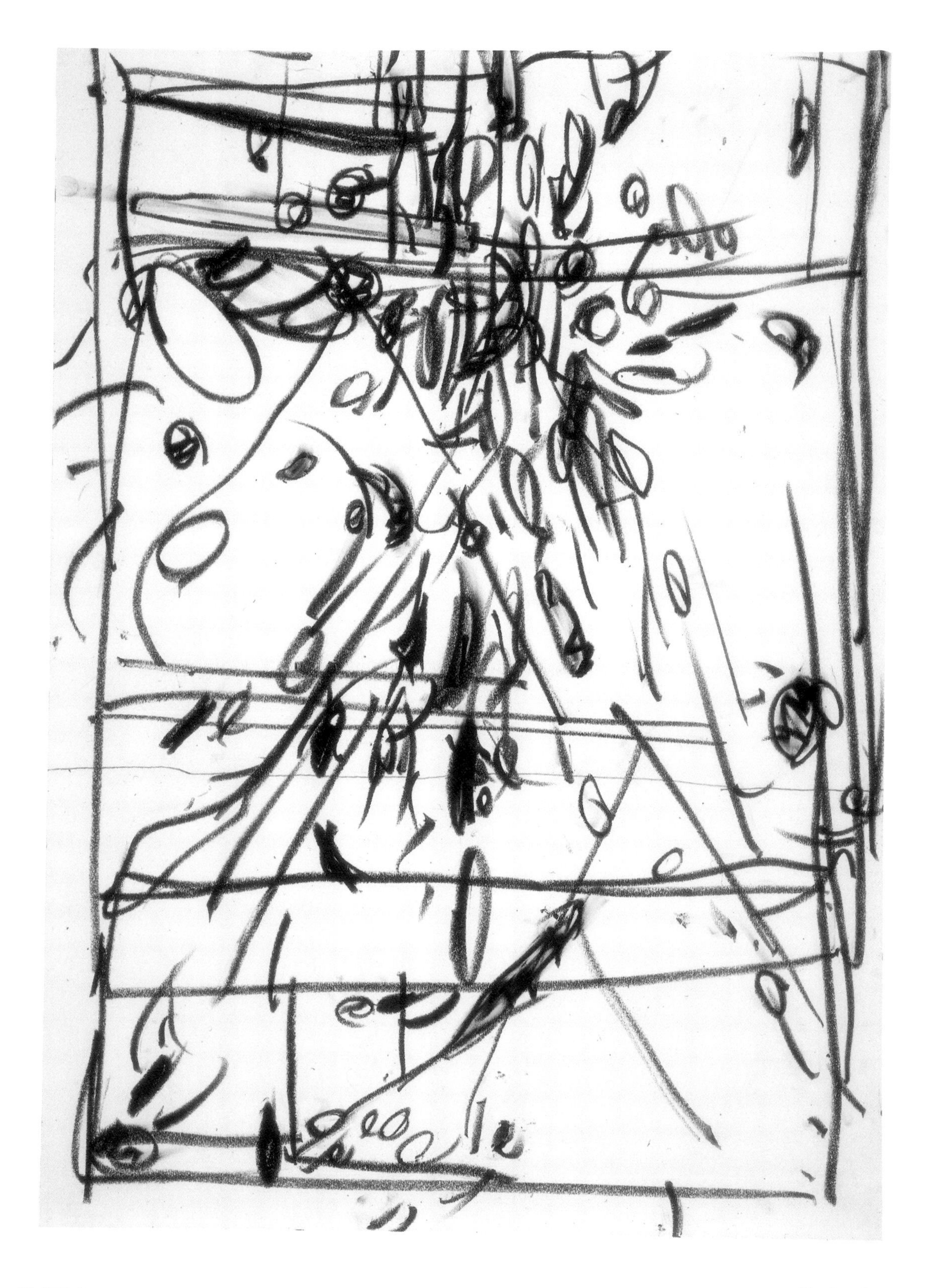

PLATE 4

Untitled, 1971
30 x 22⅛ in.
Crayon
1999.267

Untitled, 1971
30 x 22 in.
Crayon
1999.689

PLATE 5

PLATE 6

Untitled, 1971
11 x 8⅝ in.
Crayon
1999.404

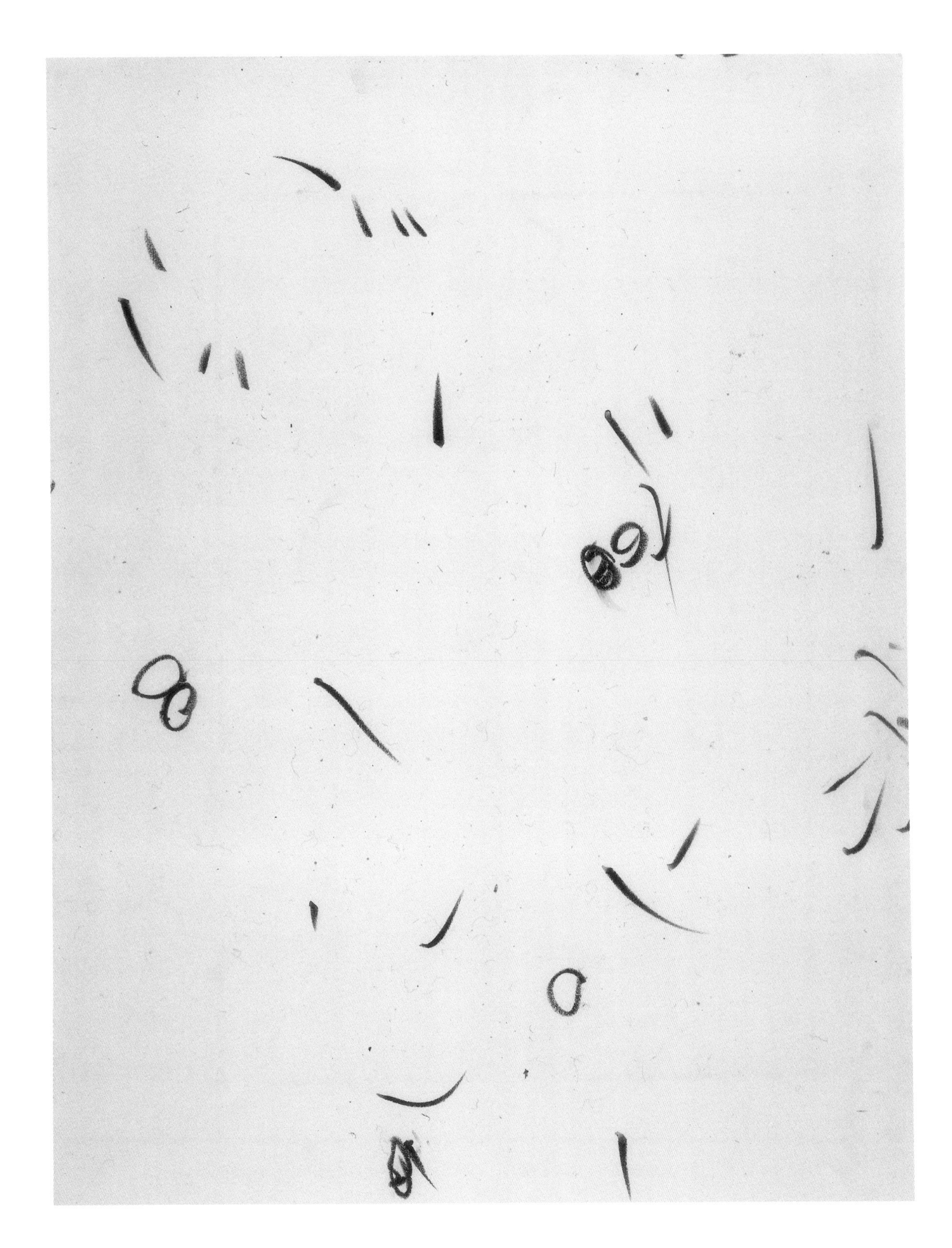

Untitled, 1972
30 x 22⅛ in.
Crayon
1999.266

PLATE 7

PLATE 8

Untitled, 1971
14 x 17 in.
Crayon, ballpoint pen,
and watercolor
1999.292

Untitled, 1971

17⅛ x 14 in.

Crayon and wash

1999.1359

PLATE 9

PLATE 10

Untitled, 1971
17 x 14 in.
Graphite, crayon, ballpoint pen, and wash
1999.1361

Untitled, 1971

11 x 14 in.

Crayon and ballpoint pen

1999.305

PLATE 11

PLATE 12

Untitled, 1970–71
25⅝ x 22½ in.
Crayon
1999.144

Untitled, 1970
28⅝ x 22⁹⁄₁₆ in.
Crayon
1999.265

PLATE 13

PLATE 14

Untitled, 1972
28⅞ x 22½ in.
Crayon
1999.141

Untitled, 1972

24 x 18 in.

Graphite, charcoal, crayon, paint,

and collage, including tape

1999.236

PLATE 16

Untitled, 1972
17⅛ x 14⅛ in.
Crayon
1999.233

Untitled, 1972

12 x 9¹⁄₁₆ in.

Graphite and crayon

1999.247

PLATE 17

PLATE 18

Untitled, 1972
12 x 9⅛ in.
Crayon
1999.246

Untitled, 1972
38 x 50 in.
Paint, crayon, graphite,
and collage, including tape
1999.621

PLATE 19

PLATE 20

Untitled, 1974
24 x 31¾ in.
Crayon, graphite, ballpoint pen, and collage, including tape
1999.383

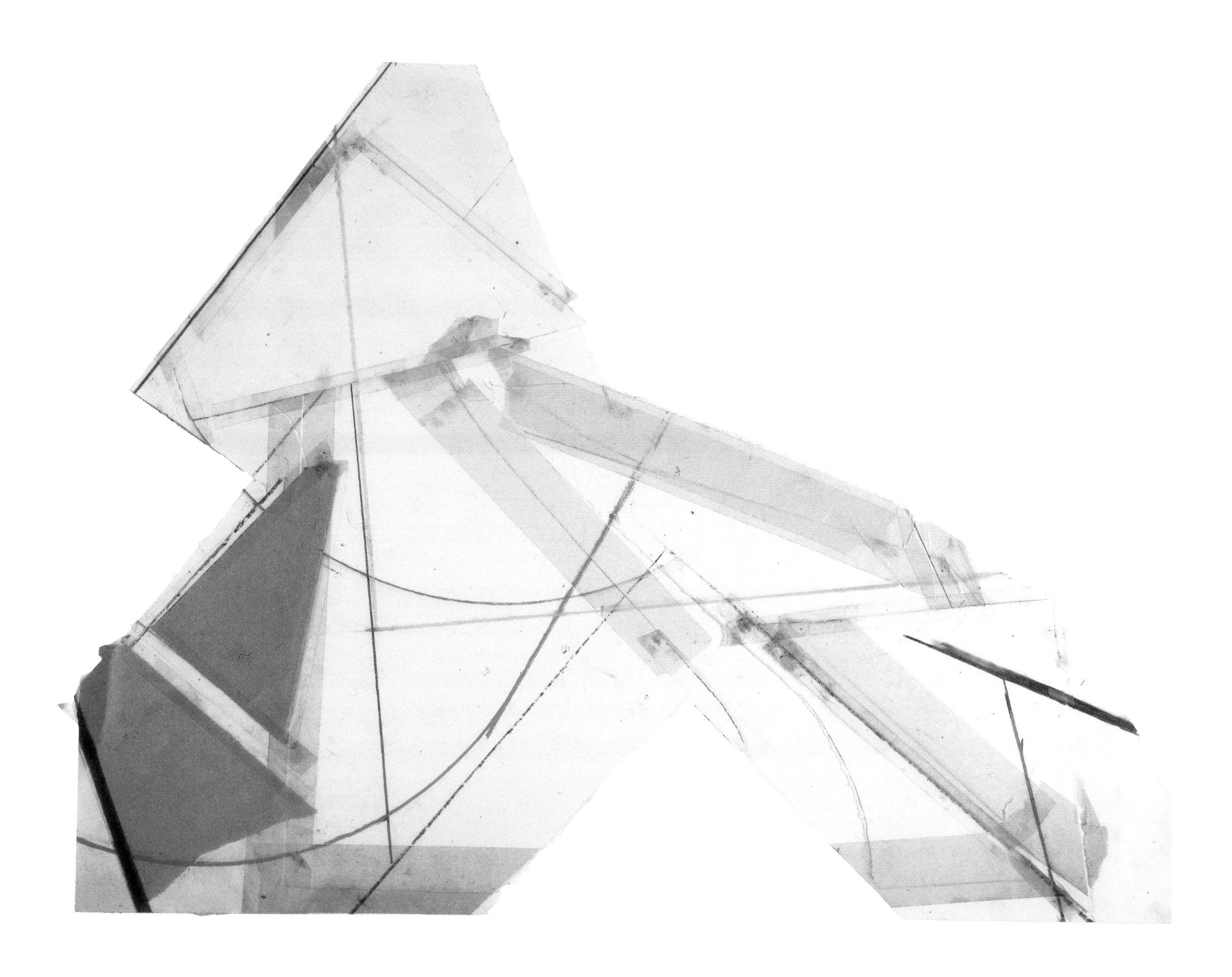

Untitled, 1974
28 x 36 in.
Crayon, graphite, and collage,
including tape
1999.614

PLATE 21

PLATE 22

Untitled, 1974
25 x 31 in.
Graphite, crayon, ballpoint pen,
and collage, including tape
1999.387

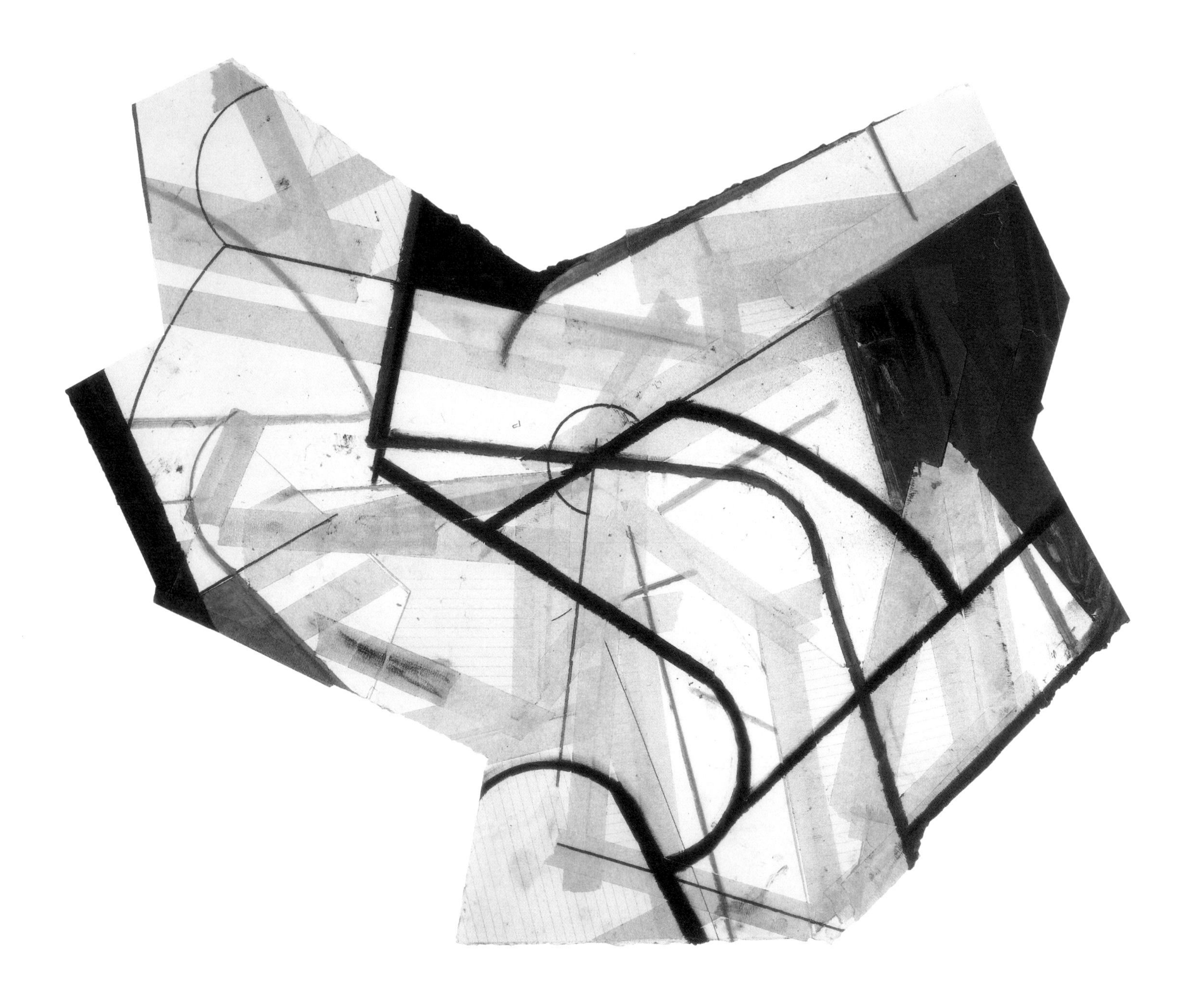

Untitled, 1974
26¾ x 28¾ in.
Graphite, paint, crayon, ballpoint pen,
and collage, including tape
1999.385

PLATE 23

PLATE 24

Untitled, 1974
28⅜ x 22¼ in.
Paint, crayon, graphite,
and collage, including tape
1999.565

Untitled, 1974

27 x 35 in.

Paint, crayon, graphite, varnish, and collage, including glue, tape, and sheets of plastic

1999.700

PLATE 25

PLATE 26

Untitled, 1974
25¼ x 39½ in.
Graphite, crayon, ballpoint pen,
and collage, including tape
1999.613

Untitled, 1974
28 x 38¼ in.
Crayon, graphite, ballpoint pen,
and collage, including tape
1999.704

PLATE 27

PLATE 28

Untitled, 1974
30⅛ x 22¼ in.
Graphite, ballpoint pen,
crayon, and wash
1999.176

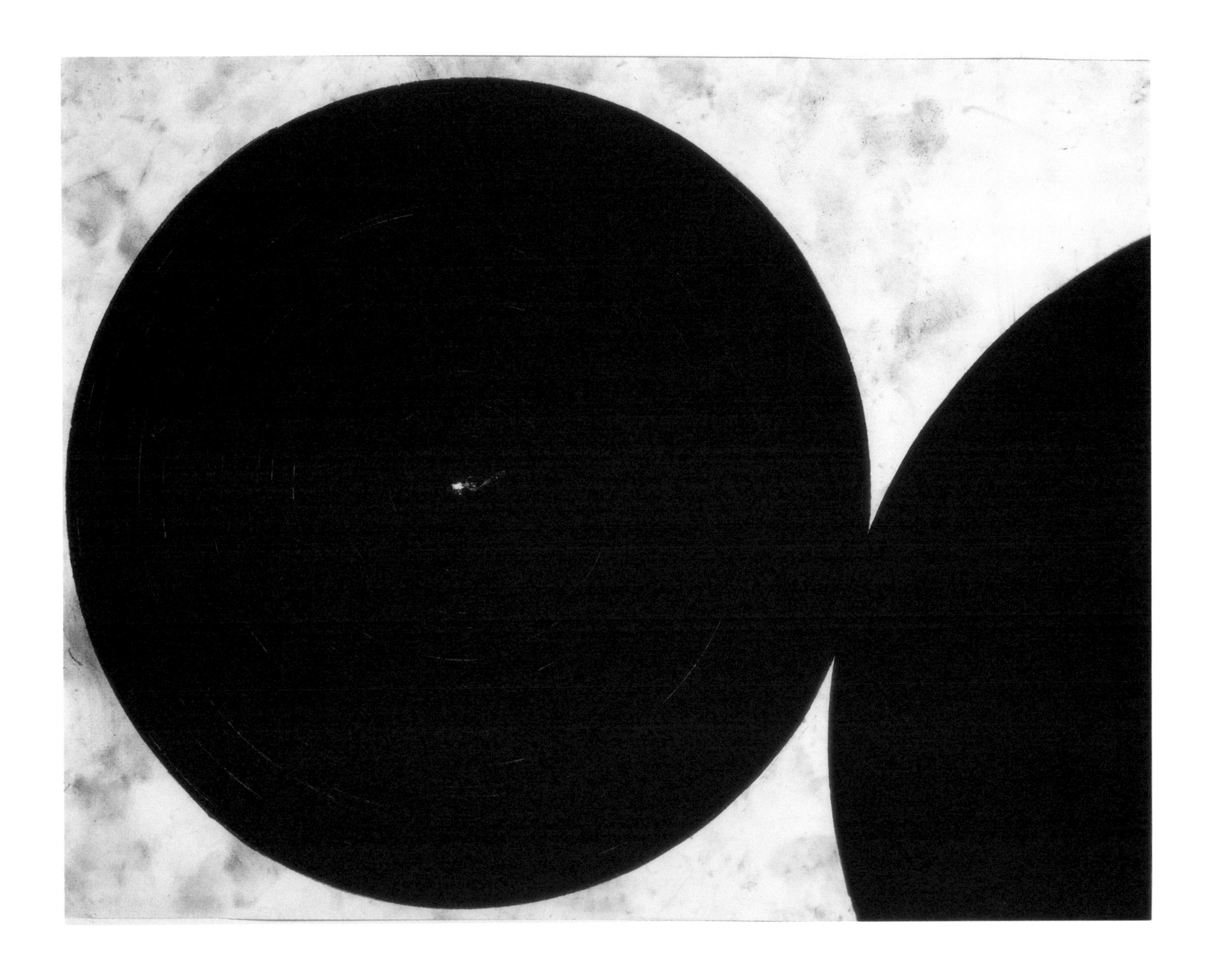

Untitled, 1974

40½ x 52⅛ in.

Graphite

1999.697

PLATE 29

PLATE 30

Study for Roller Coaster, 1977
25½ x 29⁹⁄₁₆ in.
Graphite, paint, varnish
or glue, and collage
1999.271

Roller Coaster III, 1977

38¼ x 36⅛ in.

Paint, graphite, crayon, ballpoint pen, varnish, and collage

1999.703

PLATE 31

PLATE 32

Untitled (Fuselage), 1974
22⅝ x 30¼ in.
Graphite, crayon, and collage,
including tape
1999.175

Untitled (Fuselage), 1974

21½ x 30⅛ in.

Graphite, crayon, and ballpoint pen

1999.153

PLATE 33

PLATE 34

Untitled (Fuselage), 1974
22⅞ x 30 in.
Graphite and crayon
1999.174

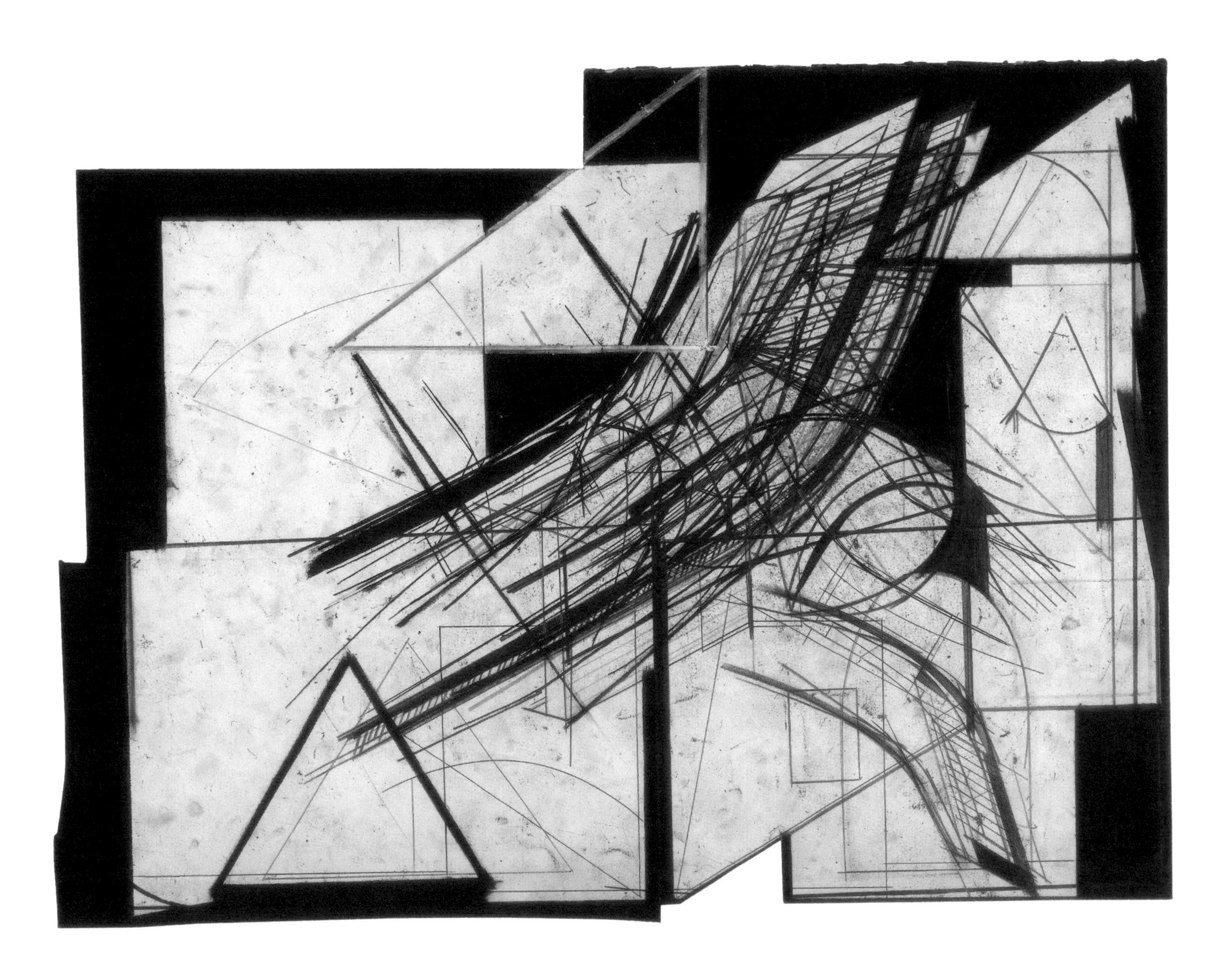

Untitled (Fuselage), 1974
22 x 29¾ in.
Graphite, crayon, ballpoint
pen, and paint
1999.152

PLATE 35

PLATE 36

Untitled (Fuselage), 1974
22¼ x 30⅛ in.
Graphite and crayon
1999.154

Untitled (Fuselage), 1974

23 x 29 in.

Graphite, crayon, and ballpoint pen

1999.147

PLATE 37

PLATE 38

Untitled (Fuselage), 1974
23 x 29 in.
Graphite, crayon, ballpoint
pen, and collage
1999.157

Untitled (Fuselage), 1974
23⅛ x 29 in.
Graphite, ballpoint pen, crayon, paint,
and collage, including tape
1999.159

PLATE 39

PLATE 40

Untitled, 1974

22 x 30⅛ in.

Graphite and ballpoint pen

1999.224

Untitled, 1975
22⅛ x 30⅛ in.
Graphite, ballpoint pen,
crayon, and wash
1999.181

PLATE 41

PLATE 42

Untitled, 1975
30 x 22⅛ in.
Graphite, crayon, ballpoint pen,
paint, and collage
1999.180

Untitled, 1975

22 x 30⅛ in.

Graphite, ballpoint pen, and collage

1999.179

PLATE 43

PLATE 44

Cast Cement, 1979
23⅛ x 29⅛ in.
Graphite, crayon, and wax
1999.362

Cast Cement, 1979

23⅛ x 29 in.

Graphite and ballpoint pen

1999.142

PLATE 45

PLATE 46

Siren, 1979

23⅛ x 29⅛ in.

Graphite, ballpoint pen, crayon,
paint, wax, and collage

1999.217

Untitled, 1979
23⅛ x 29⅛ in.
Graphite, crayon, paint,
wax, and ballpoint pen
1999.218

PLATE 47

PLATE 48

Untitled, 1979
29⅛ x 23⅛ in.
Graphite, crayon, ballpoint
pen, paint, and wax
1999.221

Untitled, 1979
29⅛ x 23⅛ in.
Graphite, crayon, paint, wax,
varnish, and ballpoint pen
1999.219

PLATE 49

PLATE 50

Holiday Cabin, 1978
23½ x 29⅛ in.
Paint, graphite, and crayon
1999.272

Cabin Circuit, 1978
22⅞ x 29⅞ in.
Graphite, crayon, paint,
wax, and collage
1999.137

PLATE 51

PLATE 52

Untitled, 1981
29⅛ x 23⅛ in.
Crayon, paint, wax,
and graphite
1999.679

Untitled, 1981
29 x 23 in.
Crayon, paint, and wax
1999.677

PLATE 53

PLATE 54

Untitled, 1981
29⅛ x 23⅛ in.
Crayon, paint, and wax
1999.678

Untitled, 1981

29⅛ x 23⅛ in.

Crayon, paint, and wax

1999.675

PLATE 55

PLATE 56

Untitled, 1981
29⅛ x 23⅛ in.
Crayon, paint, and wax
1999.423

Untitled (Marine Shelf), 1980

23 1/16 x 29 in.

Paint

1999.687

PLATE 57

PLATE 58

Untitled (Anthology), 1981
11 x 14 in.
Graphite, ballpoint pen,
crayon, wax, and collage
1999.457

Untitled (Anthology), 1981
11 x 14⅛ in.
Graphite, ballpoint pen,
crayon, wax, and collage
1999.455

PLATE 59

PLATE 60

Untitled (Anthology), 1981

10⅞ x 14¹⁄₁₆ in.

Graphite, crayon, and collage

1999.460

Untitled (Anthology), 1981
11¼ x 14 in.
Graphite, ballpoint pen,
crayon, wax, and collage
1999.461

PLATE 61

PLATE 62

Untitled (Anthology), 1981
11 x 14 in.
Graphite and collage
1999.454

Untitled (Anthology), 1981

11 x 14¹⁄₁₆ in.

Graphite, crayon, wax, and collage

1999.456

PLATE 63

PLATE 64

Untitled (Anthology), 1981
11 x 14 1/16 in.
Graphite, ballpoint pen,
crayon, wax, and collage
1999.459

Untitled (Anthology), 1981

11 x 14⅛ in.

Graphite, ballpoint pen,

crayon, and collage

1999.458

PLATE 65

PLATE 66

Untitled (Agriculture), 1990
11⅛ x 14⅛ in.
Graphite, crayon, paint,
varnish, and collage
1999.450

Untitled (Agriculture), 1991

11 1/16 x 17 in.

Graphite, crayon, paint, varnish, and collage

1999.550

PLATE 67

PLATE 68

Untitled (Agriculture), 1991
21⅞ x 15¼ in.
Graphite, crayon, paint,
varnish, and collage
1999.381

Untitled (Agriculture), 1992

11⅛ x 14⅛ in.

Graphite, crayon, paint, and varnish

1999.451

PLATE 69

PLATE 70

Untitled (Agriculture), 1992
11⅛ x 14⅛ in.
Graphite, crayon, paint,
varnish, and collage
1999.444

Untitled (Agriculture), 1990

11¼ x 14 in.

Graphite, paint, varnish, and collage

1999.445

PLATE 71

PLATE 72

Untitled (Family Tree), 1981
17 x 14 in.
Paint and wax
1999.171

Untitled (Family Tree), 1981

17 x 14 in.

Paint, collage, and wax

1999.642

PLATE 73

PLATE 74

Untitled (Family Tree), 1981
17 x 14 in.
Paint and wax
1999.671

Untitled (Family Tree), 1981

17 x 14 in.

Paint and wax

1999.672

PLATE 75

PLATE 76

Untitled (Family Tree), 1981
17 x 14 in.
Paint and wax
1999.670

Untitled (Family Tree), 1981

17 x 14 in.

Paint and wax

1999.667

PLATE 77

PLATE 78

Untitled (Warfare), 1982
23⅛ x 26½ in.
Crayon and wax
1999.389

Untitled (Warfare), 1982

22⅛ x 30⅛ in.

Crayon and wax

1999.690

PLATE 79

PLATE 80

Untitled (Warfare), 1993
22⅞ x 30 in.
Paint
1999.388

Untitled (Warfare), 1993

23¾ x 33$^{1}/_{16}$ in.

Paint, crayon, wax, and collage

1999.619

PLATE 81

PLATE 82

Untitled, 1988

17⅜ x 12 in.

Paint, varnish, and collage

1999.352

Untitled, 1988

16 x $12\frac{5}{16}$ in.

Paint, crayon, varnish, and collage

1999.317

PLATE 83

PLATE 84

Untitled, 1988

17⅛ x 14¾ in.

Paint, crayon, varnish, and collage

1999.1367

Untitled, 1988
14⅛ x 12½ in.
Paint, varnish, and collage
1999.304

PLATE 85

PLATE 86

Untitled, 1988

23⅛ x 14⅝ in.

Paint, varnish, and collage

1999.336

Untitled, 1988

23⅛ x 14⅝ in.

Paint, crayon, and varnish

1999.338

PLATE 87

PLATE 88

Untitled, 1988
23⅛ x 14½ in.
Paint, crayon, and varnish
1999.339

Untitled, 1988

23⅞ x 15⅞ in.

Paint, crayon, varnish, and collage

1999.340

PLATE 89

PLATE 90

Untitled, 1988
22½ x 15¾ in.
Paint, crayon, varnish,
glue, and collage
1999.341

Untitled, 1988
23 x 14⁹⁄₁₆ in.
Paint and varnish
1999.462

PLATE 91

PLATE 92

Untitled, 1988
14 x 11¼ in.
Paint, varnish, and collage
1999.363

Untitled, ca. 1988

18⅝ x 14⅞ in.

Paint, varnish, and collage

1999.554

PLATE 93

PLATE 94

Untitled, 1989
14¼ x 11 in.
Paint, crayon, and varnish
1999.557

Untitled, 1990

14⅛ x 11 in.

Crayon, paint, varnish, and collage

1999.286

PLATE 95

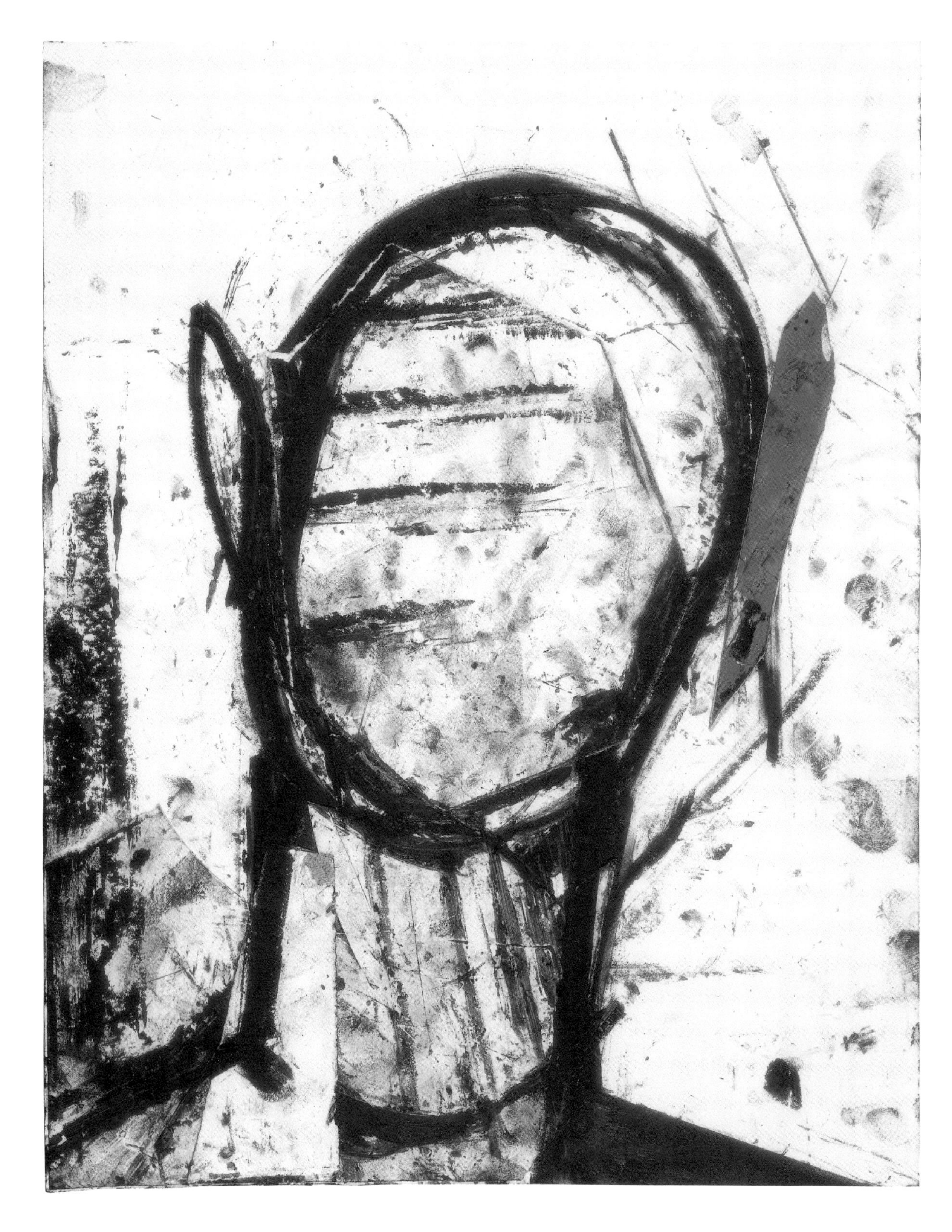

PLATE 96

Untitled, 1990
16⅝ x 11¼ in.
Crayon, paint, wax, and collage
1999.491

Untitled, 1990
14 x 11 1⁄16 in.
Graphite, crayon, paint,
wax, and collage
1999.490

PLATE 97

PLATE 98

Untitled, 1990
14 x 11 in.
Crayon, paint, varnish, and collage
1999.314

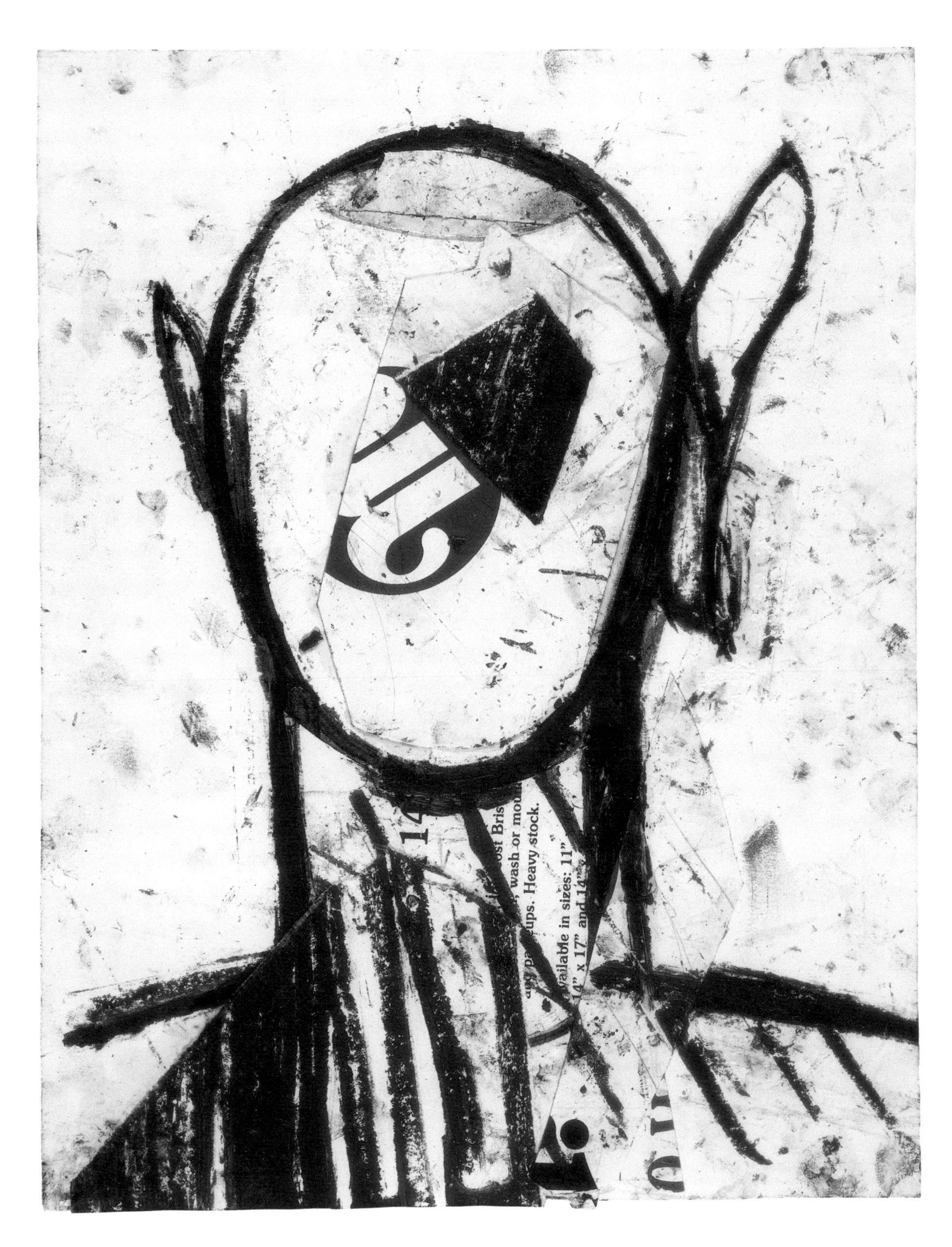

Untitled, 1990

PLATE 99

14⅛ x 11 in.

Crayon, paint, wax, and collage

1999.507

PLATE 100

Untitled, 1990–91

16⅜ x 12⅛ in.

Crayon, paint, varnish, and collage

1999.555

Untitled, 1994
29⅛ x 23⅛ in.
Graphite, paint, crayon,
varnish, and collage
1999.584

PLATE 101

PLATE 102

Untitled, 1994
16 x 11⅝ in.
Graphite, crayon, paint,
varnish, and collage
1999.562

Untitled, 1994

PLATE 103

21⅝ x 15⅜ in.

Paint, varnish, and collage

1999.544

PLATE 104

Untitled, 1994

19⅞ x 12¼ in.

Crayon, paint, varnish, and collage

1999.561

Untitled, 1994
14¼ x 11⅞ in.
Graphite, paint, varnish, and collage
1999.312

PLATE 105

PLATE 106

Untitled, 1995
17⅞ x 14⅛ in.
Paint, varnish, and collage
1999.546

Untitled, 1995

17⅛ x 12⅝ in.

Paint, crayon, varnish, and collage

1999.474

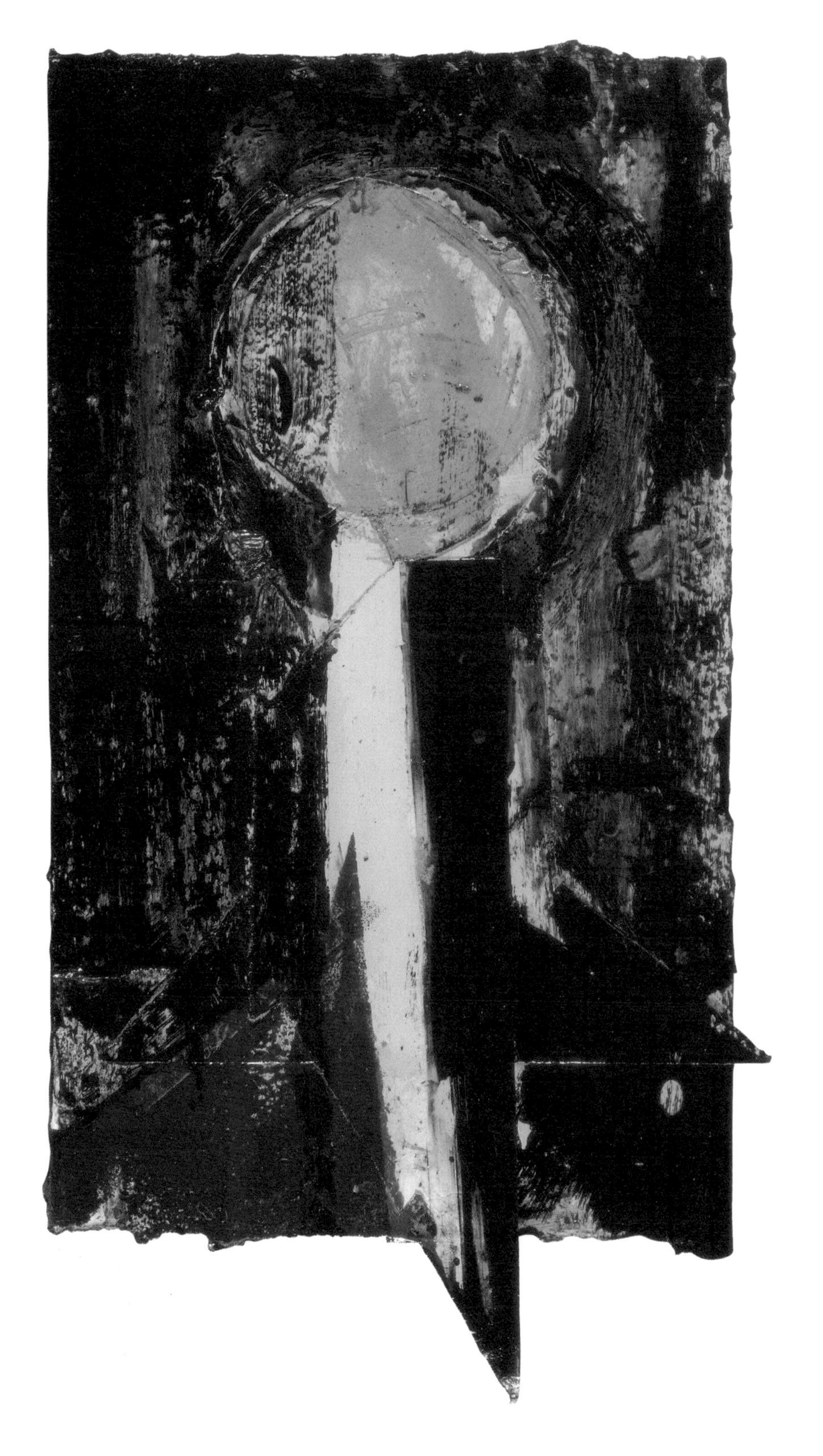

PLATE 108

Untitled, ca. 1994

23½ x 13 in.

Crayon, paint, varnish, and collage

1999.541

Untitled, 1995

21⅛ x 14⅜ in.

Paint, varnish, and collage

1999.543

PLATE 109

PLATE 110

Untitled, 1995–96

23½ x 13 in.

Crayon, graphite, paint, and varnish

1999.547

Untitled, 1994–95

33½ x 33¼ in.

Graphite, crayon, paint, varnish, and collage

1999.626

PLATE 111

PLATE 112

Untitled (On the Thames, English Cottage), 1984
17 x 14 in.
Paint, crayon, wax, and graphite
1999.650

Untitled (On the Thames, English Cottage), 1984

PLATE 113

17 x 14 in.

Paint, crayon, wax, and graphite

1999.655

PLATE 114

Untitled (On the Thames, English Cottage), 1984

17 x 14 in.

Paint, crayon, wax, and graphite

1999.198

Untitled (On the Thames, English Cottage), 1984

17 x 14 in.

Paint, crayon, wax, and graphite

1999.649

PLATE 115

PLATE 116

Untitled (On the Thames, English Cottage), 1984
17 x 14 in.
Paint, crayon, and wax
1999.662

Untitled (On the Thames, English Cottage), 1984

17 x 14 in.

Paint, crayon, and wax

1999.648

PLATE 117

PLATE 118

Untitled (On the Thames, English Cottage), 1985–86
17 x 14 in.
Paint, varnish, and collage on two overlayed
sheets of plastic and one sheet of paper
1999.276

Untitled (On the Thames, English Cottage), 1991

17 x 14 in.

Graphite, crayon, paint,

varnish, and collage

1999.598

PLATE 119

PLATE 120

Untitled (On the Thames, English Cottage), 1992

30⅞ x 13⅞ in.

Graphite, crayon, paint,

wax, and collage

1999.576

Untitled (On the Thames, English Cottage), 1992

30¼ x 13⅞ in.

Graphite, crayon, paint, and collage

1999.575

PLATE 121

PLATE 122

Winter, 1992–93

30¼ x 22¼ in.

Paint, crayon, and varnish

1999.583

Gordon Newton

Born 1948, Detroit, Michigan

Education:

Wayne State University, Detroit, 1971-72

Society of Arts and Crafts, Detroit, 1969

Port Huron Community College, Michigan

Grants:

1983 Michigan Council for the Arts, Creative Artist Grant

1981 National Endowment for the Arts, Creative Artist Grant

Michigan Council for the Arts, Creative Artist Grant

1979 National Endowment for the Arts Fellowship

Awards:

1986 Awards in the Visual Arts 5, The Equitable Life Assurance Society and the Rockefeller Foundation

1982 Michigan Foundation for the Arts Award

1970 Mr. & Mrs. Lester B. Arwin Purchase Prize and Detroit Artists Market Prize

Solo Exhibitions:

1989 "Marine Light Series 1987-88," Joy Emery Gallery, Grosse Pointe Farms, Michigan

"Love, Life, Geometric Heritage 1988-1989," Susanne Hilberry Gallery, Birmingham, Michigan; shared catalogue with "Marine Light Series"

1983 "Gordon Newton," Feigenson Gallery, Detroit

1973 "Gordon Newton," J. L. Hudson Gallery, Detroit

Selected Group Exhibitions:

1999 "Back Room Exhibition," Susanne Hilberry Gallery

1998 "Assemblage," Center Galleries, Center for Creative Studies, Detroit

Selected Group Exhibitions: (continued)

1998 "A Sustaining Passion: The Tsagaris/Hilberry Collection," Cedar Rapids Museum of Art, Cedar Rapids, Iowa; Dubuque Museum of Art, Iowa; with catalogue

1997 "Salient Green," Susanne Hilberry Gallery

1996 "Black and Blue," Susanne Hilberry Gallery

1994 "Group Exhibition," Susanne Hilberry Gallery

1993 "Group Exhibition," Susanne Hilberry Gallery

1991 "Drawings," Susanne Hilberry Gallery

1986-87 "Awards in the Visual Arts 5," Neuberger Museum of Art, State University of New York–Purchase; Columbus Museum of Art, Ohio; Norton Gallery and School of Art, West Palm Beach, Florida; with catalogue

"Michigan NEA Fellowship 1965-85," Detroit Focus Gallery

"Art on Paper," Weatherspoon Gallery, University of North Carolina—Greensboro

1984 "Contemporary Art in the Collection of Florence and S. Brooks Barron," Meadow Brook Art Gallery, Oakland University, Rochester, Michigan; with catalogue

1982 "Guts," Herron School of Art Gallery, Indiana University, Indianapolis

1980-81 "Kick Out the Jams: Detroit's Cass Corridor, 1963-1977," The Detroit Insitute of Arts; Museum of Contemporary Art, Chicago; with catalogue

1979 "Art Inc.: American Paintings from Corporate Collections," Montgomery Museum of Fine Arts, Alabama; with catalogue

"At Cranbrook: Downtown Detroit—Twenty-one Artists," Cranbrook Academy of Art Museum, Bloomfield Hills, Michigan; with catalogue

(CONTINUED)

Selected Group Exhibitions: (continued)

1978 "Young American Artists: Exxon National Exhibition," The Solomon R. Guggenheim Museum, New York; with catalogue

1973 "American Drawings," Whitney Museum of American Art, New York; with catalogue

1972 "Twelve Statements beyond the '60's," The Detroit Institute of Arts; with catalogue

1970 "58th Exhibition for Michigan Artists," The Detroit Institute of Arts; with catalogue

Selected Bibliography:

1987 John Barron, "Newton's Universe," Detroit Monthly 11, 3 (March): 88-95

1979 Jay Belloli, "New Faces/New Images," Ocular Magazine, 4, 4 (Winter): 38

1978 Robert Pincus Witten, "Detroit Notes: Islands in Blight," Arts Magazine 52 (February): 127-143

Exhibition Reviews:

1998 Joy Hakanson Colby, "It's Another Scrappy Show for Center Galleries," The Detroit News, June 4

1989 Corinne Abatt, "Heads Show Newton's Skill," The Eccentric Newspapers, May 25

Joy Hakanson Colby, "Detroit Art Community has Two Reasons to Cheer," The Detroit News, May 5

Exhibition Reviews: (continued)

Marsha Miro, "The Gritty Art of Motown's Best is Back," Detroit Free Press, May 4

Gilda Snowden, "Gordon Newton," Detroit Focus Quarterly 8, 1-2 (spring-summer)

1985 Marsha Miro, "Exhibit Touched by a Sense of the Soul," Detroit Free Press, February 24

Joy Hakanson Colby, "The Figure in Wood, Bronze...and Neon?" The Detroit News, February 10

1983 Marsha Miro, "Fresh Visions of Originality," Detroit Free Press, November 20

Dennis Alan Nawrocki, "Gordon Newton," New Art Examiner, June

Marsha Miro, "Brillant Show Weds Order, Disorder," Detroit Free Press, April 22

Joy Hakanson Colby, "Structo-Vision," The Detroit News, April 10

1982 Marsha Miro, "Industrial Wreckage Fuels Cass Artists' Imaginations," Detroit Free Press, October 3

———, "Unique Images of Detroit," Detroit Free Press, July 15

John Russell, "Art: Young Americans at the Guggenheim," The New York Times, May 12

1973 Joy Hakanson [Colby], "2 Successes in New Mediums," The Detroit News, February 11